Forbes®

BEST
BUSINESS
MISTAKES

How Today's Top Business Leaders
Turned Missteps into Success

BOB SELLERS

WILEY

John Wiley & Sons, Inc.

Published by John Wiley & Sons, Inc., Hoboken, New Jersey.
FORBES is a registered trademark of Forbes LLC. Its use is pursuant to a license agreement.
Published simultaneously in Canada.

For general information on our other products and services or for technical support, please contact our Customer Care Department within the United States at (800) 762-2974, outside the United States at (317) 572-3993 or fax (317) 572-4002.

Wiley also publishes its books in a variety of electronic formats. Some content that appears in print may not be available in electronic books. For more information about Wiley products, visit our web site at www.wiley.com.

Library of Congress Cataloging-in-Publication Data:

Sellers, Bob, 1955–

  Forbes best business mistakes: how today's top business leaders turned missteps into success / Bob Sellers.
    p. cm.
  ISBN 978-0-470-59877-1 (pbk.)
    1. Decision making.   2. Errors.   3. Success in business.   4. Management.   I. Title.
  HD30.23.S447 2010
  658.4′03—dc22

                                                            2010005943

Printed in the United States of America

10 9 8 7 6 5 4 3 2 1

Contents

Acknowledgments

First, let me thank my wife, Anna. She always waits to see whether winners of Oscars or Emmys will mention their spouses, so I figured I'd better get that out of the way. She's still the best thing to ever come out of Texas. (Tex-Mex is second, with Lyle Lovett and Joe Ely tied for third.)

I also would like to acknowledge the guidance and support from my John Wiley & Sons editor, Laura Walsh. First, she believed in the project, and then she provided the energy to drive it every step of the way. Without exception she was a ray of sunshine. It was a blessing to have an editor who felt like a friend even as she was doing her job as a professional.

I would also like to thank each of the participants for taking a chance on a topic that not everybody wants to talk about. I hope the profiles and my treatment of their stories warranted their trust and commitment to the project. And of course I want to extend my appreciation to Steve Forbes, whose company has seen fit to put its name on the book. For more than 90 years, the brand has earned widespread respect, and I consider it a privilege to try to live up to those standards.

Finally, there are two little girls who were often told in recent months, "Not now, girls, maybe later. Daddy's working on his book."

This is later.

About the Author

B ob Sellers has worked as a journalist for 20 years, including nine as an anchor at the national level with CNBC and Fox News Channel. At CNBC, he anchored three hours a day and reported on Wall Street during the dot-com buildup and collapse. At FNC he anchored daytime programs covering general news and international politics, interviewing everyone from Benjamin Netanyahu to Mikhail Gorbachev, and reported live from Baghdad in the early stages of the Iraq war in 2003. As a television anchor and general assignment reporter he has worked in Medford, Oregon; San Antonio, Texas; Seattle, Washington; and Washington, D.C. His columns have appeared in various magazines and newspapers, and he has worked as a financial consultant for Merrill Lynch and Shearson Lehman Hutton. He has appeared as a financial guest on CNBC and Fox Business Network, and has contributed to public radio's Marketplace Radio. He was drafted to play professional baseball out of high school by the Kansas City Royals, but chose to attend the University of Virginia instead. He has served on the Board of Advisors for the University's Media Studies Department. He now lives in Nashville with his wife, Anna, and their twin daughters. His web site is Bobsellers.net.

Introduction

Mistakes.

We all make them. There's nothing more personal, and nothing more powerful than the lessons taken from them. If you don't believe me, just ask some of the most accomplished people in America. That's exactly what I did in *Forbes Best Business Mistakes: How Today's Top Business Leaders Turned Missteps into Success.*

The strange thing is that these folks willingly talked to me about their missteps. I've worked for some of the biggest corporations and most successful television networks in the country and I've discovered that almost nobody else wants to talk about them. At least not in a positive way.

When you're at a dinner party or gathering of professional colleagues, you don't hear someone brag about how they made a huge mistake and it helped get them where they are today. No aspiring top-level executive is going to tap his fork against his wine glass to get the room's attention and then launch into a recounting of a monumental misstep that led to his professional demise—and his ultimate phoenixlike rise from the ashes to professional heights due to the lessons learned from a career blunder.

No, you usually hear about how smart someone is—about how they made a deft decision or arranged a crafty deal or picked an unknown stock that soared beyond anyone's expectations. But it might be a more valuable story to hear what went wrong. From talking to the people in this book, I've concluded that making mistakes and learning from them is an essential part of the process that leads to success.

Mohamed El-Erian, the PIMCO executive who once managed Harvard University's endowment, told me about the value he's seen in other people's experience. "I've learned from other people's mistakes," he said, and that's why he was willing to talk to me about *his.* "No one goes through life without making mistakes. Life is too unpredictable and we are imperfect instruments to deal with life. The important thing is not to make the same mistake over and over again. Recognize that it's not the end of the world if you make a mistake—these things happen. What is problematic is when you don't *learn* from the mistake."

Or as Winston Churchill said, "All men make mistakes, but only wise men learn from their mistakes."

Success in a business career—any career, really—doesn't happen because everything falls into place. For the Olympic athlete standing on the medal platform, success didn't come from just showing up on the day of the competition. There were years of putting in the hard work and learning from doing something over and over again and making corrections to what goes drastically wrong and tiny adjustments to what needs refining. And then there's the challenge of doing it when it counts. There's virtually no activity, athletic or otherwise, in which trial and error doesn't play a role. Why would a business career be any different?

"I've met successful people all over the world," Dave Ramsey told me, "athletes, artists, and people who have huge ministries, people who are known on television or whatever, and we perceive their success as somehow being linear, from point A to point B, just a straight line up the mountain. And the truth is it's a whole life full of fits and starts. It's a life full of course corrections. It's a life full of bumps on the head so you learn where to not put your head again."

Most of the people in this book were like the rest of us, working in comparative obscurity. They hadn't become household names. They weren't on the podium hoisting their gold medals in triumphant celebration for the world to see. They were putting in years of grinding and grueling work to master their professions, training themselves to deal with the obstacles they confronted, and at the ultimate moments of challenge, when they could apply the lessons they had learned through failure, they summoned the best of themselves, made the right decisions, and emerged with consequential career achievements.

And there's something else the people I talked to shared: a focused and unrelenting drive, which is probably why their mistakes couldn't throw them off track permanently. The attitude reminded me of the late football coach Vince Lombardi. He coached the Green Bay Packers to five league titles in nine years, including victories in the first two Super Bowls. He taught his teams to never give up. When they lost a game, he would say, "We didn't lose the game; we just ran out of time." It was reflection of Lombardi's relentless will to succeed. "The difference between a successful person and others is not a lack of strength, not a lack of knowledge, but rather a lack of will." The Super Bowl's top prize is now called the Vince Lombardi Trophy.

"Best" Mistakes

Oh sure, there are books about mistakes. Most are about how to *avoid* them. You can find books on how to avoid mistakes in buying a house, picking a mate, writing a novel, investing your individual retirement account (IRA), putting on makeup, sailing a boat, speaking Italian, selling a product, speaking in public, getting into college, interviewing for a job, pursuing a legal case, managing subordinates, running a medical practice—even choosing a horse.

But you don't see too many books about why making mistakes is a positive, perhaps necessary, step toward success.

"Successful people learn from their mistakes," says Dr. Georgia Witkin, clinical psychiatrist at Mount Sinai Medical Center in New York. It sounds simple, but it's not. She says most people avoid the risk taking needed to succeed, because they can't handle failure. "People who reach the top of their fields embrace mistakes because the lessons they learn allow them to get closer to their goals. It's what sets them apart."

That's not to say all mistakes are good. In the corporate world, there was Ford's Edsel back in the 1950s and Betamax and New Coke in the 1980s; the Internet era had an abundance of them, though Pets.com and its screwy sock puppet readily comes to mind; and in recent years there was Jay Leno in prime time. But in all fairness, even those screwups contained lessons for somebody (wherever they are).

When I lived in Los Angeles I used to go down to Venice Beach over the Fourth of July weekend and watch all the crazy people come out. There was a guy there who would juggle *running* chain saws. Chain saws! How do you master *that* through trial and error? I always wondered if there was another guy with just one arm who juggled chain saws—was he better or worse than the guy with two arms? That wouldn't be a good mistake. Two mistakes and you're pretty much done.

And some mistakes are so big and personally destructive that no matter who you are, you wouldn't want to share them. Those aren't the kinds of things I wanted to know about from the participants in this book. I wanted to know about the *good* mistakes, the ones that contained true value.

The best mistakes here beat others in the value they provide. The business leaders share stories of missteps that provided opportunities for them to succeed. It could have been an event that taught them an enduring lesson, or a blunder that proved a natural step toward their eventual achievement. Or it could have been an experience that had the appearance to virtually everyone else of being a mistake, though they knew down deep that it wasn't—even if it took years before it became apparent to others.

Parts of the Book

In some cases, mistakes allow a person to define themselves.

Take John (Jack) Bogle, the legendary Wall Street manager and founder of Vanguard. He made a career mistake that cost him his job leading the Wellington Management Company back in the 1970s. Did he go find a hole to crawl into? No. He invented the stock index mutual fund. Nothing like creating a revenue generator that brings in hundreds of billions of dollars to put you back in good graces with the company.

"My best mistake was my biggest mistake," he told me. "I got fired, but I lived and I learned."

And there's Jack Welch, picked by *Fortune* magazine as the "Manager of the Century." Early in his career he was working with a group of chemists conducting an experiment when something went wrong and they blew the roof off the building! Instead of being fired, the incident helped catapult his career at General Electric.

The two Jacks, Welch and Bogle, lead off the **"Legends and Gurus"** part of this book. Their storytelling ability is fused with the insight that comes from decades of management experience. Like the old commercial for E.F. Hutton, when they talk, people listen. No one would deny Peter Lynch membership in that club, and he tells a story about a stock investment decision that changed the way he evaluates his investment positions.

And there are new faces in business leadership as well, like Jason Kilar at Hulu. His best mistake came from an event involving Jeff Bezos, his former boss at Amazon.com. Jason is part of **"The Next Generation"** of leaders, people who are poised to take the reins from those who came before them. Jim Buckmaster of Craigslist is in that group. He made what many saw as a mistake on a personal level that changed his life for the better—but the payoff didn't come for another 10 years.

Meredith Whitney is included in the group of new leaders as well, since she has learned to pick stocks with the best on Wall Street, even if that means going against the grain and being contrarian. The will to blaze your own path is part of what good leaders are made of, and she's young enough and driven enough to set an example for those who follow her.

There are **"Personalities"** like Mark Cuban, who says he never would have succeeded to the level he did and become a billionaire if it weren't for something that went wrong with a wet T-shirt contest. Yes, a wet T-shirt contest.

Jim Cramer, the over-the-top CNBC host who made millions as a successful hedge fund manager, reveals a "colossal mistake" that helped him turn his firm around. And Suze Orman failed to follow her own gut feeling and extended trust to someone she felt she shouldn't. It was a million-dollar mistake. "That led to the best lesson that I have stuck with to this day," she says.

I've also included **"Chief Executives,"** who may or may not be CEOs, who have managed people and programs that matter—like Arthur Blank, who launched The Home Depot along with Bernie Marcus. His misstep could be studied by every business student looking for a blueprint on how to expand a successful business beyond the local zip codes.

And Dr. Bill Frist, the former U.S. Senate majority leader, helped set up the organ transplant program at Vanderbilt University. He was there when heart transplants were in their infancy. "Every time you cured one problem," he says, "there was a new problem." The lessons learned from mistakes in that endeavor actually save lives.

Barbara Corcoran, star of ABC's *Shark Tank*, recounts a misstep that helped her become one of the biggest realtors in New York City: "I found a lesson that if you think 'How the hell do I make something good out of this?' all you need is to push a tiny bit more, that tiny 5 or 10 percent, to find something good."

First the Pain, Then the Lesson

There are motivational speakers, of course, who will talk about dealing positively with missteps. But a lot of those speakers are people you've never heard of, or haven't reached the levels of the participants in this book. I would rather learn how to hit a baseball from a major leaguer than a guy who hit .200 in the minors. (Although if that guy's Michael Jordan, I might want some advice on running the triangle offense.) There's nothing like hearing from the most accomplished businesspeople on how to deal with mistakes in a positive way.

Perhaps a perfect example is how Dave Ramsey took financial failure and turned it into a successful career. He didn't become an expert on bankruptcy and foreclosure and taking control of your financial life by coincidence. He lost everything himself and had to put it all back together. He made a fortune *twice*. He made millions investing in real estate and then lost it all when the bank called his loans. It reached a point where creditors were phoning and asking his wife how she could stay with a loser who wouldn't pay his bills.

"Pain is a thorough teacher," he told me. "You don't forget. And the deeper the pain, the more thorough the lesson." But what makes Dave Ramsey stand out is that he not only dealt with his situation and got back on track financially, but he actually built a successful business *based* on it.

That is embracing a mistake.

Dr. JoAnn Dahlkoettner, a psychologist and former world-class athlete who works with athletes and business professionals in the San Francisco Bay Area, says that mistakes are an opportunity to learn.

"The wrong way to deal with a mistake is wallowing in the 'why?' 'Why do I always do this?' Instead," she says, "you need an empowering question. 'What can I learn from this?' 'How can I deal with this next time?' 'What's the next step?' 'What *did* work?' Think about what you did when you *were* successful."

And she points out that you should avoid equating the mistake with *you*. "This has nothing to do with your value as a human being. Life is much bigger than this."

Henry Ford never would have arrived at the Model T if he had given up after his first try, or his second, or his third. The car changed American life, but only because he learned from what went wrong and then got it right.

Since so many of the participants here are in highly competitive fields, I thought they might want to avoid talking about mistakes because mistakes could be perceived as a sign of weakness, like a smile on a New York City subway train. On the contrary. They talked freely, and it's probably because they focused on the lessons. And those lessons could come in even the most unexpected places.

Bill Gross, Mohamed El-Erian's colleague at PIMCO, told me about the lessons he learned playing blackjack that enabled him to become one of the best bond money managers on the planet. Can you learn how to invest money while you're gambling? Apparently so.

Arianna Huffington, founder of the HuffingtonPost.com, learned a big lesson while standing on the same stage as the political behemoths William F. Buckley and John Kenneth Galbraith. It's an experience that still informs her activities in the field of political discussion.

Who Would Appreciate This Book

If you're someone who works in what we might call the business or corporate world, you probably already recognize many of these names and know something about them. You'll appreciate their experiences, their stories, and their lessons. Some of the lessons you could directly apply in your own career or professional endeavors.

But the stories and lessons are universal. When Suze Orman refuses the lay blame for a costly mistake on the person who stole from her—"I allowed all this to happen; I created the situation to allow this person to do me in"—you don't have to be a Harvard MBA to appreciate it.

As a television journalist I think I've developed a sixth sense of when I'm losing someone's attention on the air. I've tried to apply that sense here. I kept from getting too technical, especially with Wall Street folks like Robert Prechter and William O'Neil, who have made a living talking about things like Fibonacci retracements and relative strength.

Back when I used to do business interviews and someone would mention a stock's price-earnings (P/E) ratio, I could feel a reactionary click of remotes. Not everybody would be lost—and certainly not some of the hard-core business viewers watching CNBC—but enough of their eyes were probably glazing over that I could feel it. So I would explain that P/E is the price of a stock divided by its earnings. It means how much someone would have to pay to get a dollar in earnings. The bigger the number, the more you have to pay to get earnings. A $20 stock with a dollar in yearly earnings per share has a 20 P/E. A 10 P/E is a better buy if everything else is the same.

Now, an astute viewer could argue that I'm leaving out many other elements, such as what industry the company was in (some industries run higher P/Es), whether I was talking about trailing earnings or forward earnings, and what the future was expected to hold. That's all true, but that kind of discussion would leave a lot of people out. I've tried not to do that here.

I've tried to maintain a sense for when you might click your remote, turn off your Kindle, or decide to check your e-mail or Facebook account. And you don't have to be a businessperson (whatever that is) to appreciate the stories and lessons.

Inspirational Profiles

I've interviewed a lot of people over the past two decades, but I've never gotten fresher, less rehearsed answers than on this topic. Most business leaders are accustomed to answering questions about their successes, so they've gotten pretty good at putting them together into polished stories. They've even gotten adept at defending their company missteps when stockholders or journalists try to hold them accountable. But in talking about their mistakes in a positive way—not their worst ones or the biggest ones, but their *best* ones—I've heard stories so personal that in some cases it's like listening to secrets. And in a way, they are. In some cases this is the first time they've talked about these experiences in public.

One recurring theme that I found in talking to the participants was the habit of following their gut. And their common advice to others was to do the same.

It could be that your gut feeling, that inner voice, guides you to be in the right place at the right time to combine your talents with the perfect opportunity like some cosmic intelligence compels birds to fly south for the winter. I'm not a psychologist or a self-help guru, so I'll leave the interpretation to others.

But an interesting element in the stories here is that even when these leaders followed their gut, it didn't mean that their life or business career put them on a smooth path. It didn't lead to a professional track of achievement attained on cruise control. There were many cases in which following their gut led to financial or professional turmoil. But the consensus was that eventually—and it could be many years later—trusting that gut feeling turned out to be the right choice. It might be because if you follow that inner voice, you will always be committed to what you are doing.

I hope that you will find an inspirational value to reading these profiles. The stories can help you see that something positive can come out of blunders, even big ones. And anybody who has seen tough times in the recent economy—and that's an overwhelming majority of us—can gain something from seeing the most successful among us discuss how they applied the lessons learned through failure in order to achieve greater success.

Part One
Legends and Gurus

There are many business leaders with significant accomplishments and stories that deserve respect, so how do you define a legend or guru?

For the purposes of this book, it's kind of a Hall of Fame based on accomplishments and reputations established in the business world (as opposed to still working on it). No one could deny that Jack Welch belongs, or Jack Bogle, who created an investment product virtually every investor has utilized. The folks here wouldn't have to work another day and they'd still be known for something they've done or accomplished.

I've also included Wall Street gurus who have made their reputations on the Street. They might even still be plying their trade (or trades), but will always be known for their accomplished financial wizardry, either over the long haul or at a memorable time in the nation's financial history (like Robert Prechter predicting the 1987 crash). Peter Lynch, with his phenomenal record running Fidelity's Magellan Fund, is certainly a guru, right? And that must mean that Bill Gross of the Pacific Investment Management Company (PIMCO) is as well, since he's often called the Peter Lynch of bonds. You get the gist.

The participants here all draw on a wealth of information and experience that is valuable to those of us with much to learn. You can argue over the inclusion of any particular individual, and many other business leaders in this book could have been added to this group, but frankly the book's chapters would be too lopsided. The ultimate purpose is to recognize a level of business acumen or wisdom that at some point in a career was manifested by their business decisions, so we want to hear what they have to say. Think of Yoda in a suit.

Chapter 1
JACK WELCH

CEO of General Electric Company (GE), 1981 to 2001

Named "Manager of the Century" by *Fortune* magazine

BS, MS, and PhD in chemical engineering

I worked for Jack Welch for four years. He was running GE when I was anchoring at CNBC. This may be hard to recall, but NBC was the number one broadcast network then. Must-see TV dominated the Thursday night lineup. The *Tonight Show* was number one in its time slot, with no host controversy. CNBC was the number one cable network and even then was making more than $300 million a year. And this was all in a division that was pretty much a sideline business for the conglomerate. But Jack was quoted as saying, "You don't sell beachfront property." Since Jack left, there has been erosion on that beach.

Being number one was not a coincidence. Jack always told us he made it a policy that every business endeavor in which GE was active would have to be number one or a strong number two in order for the corporation to stay committed to it.

Strong leadership was never in question when Jack Welch was at the helm. Everyone knew who was in charge. His business savvy and wise guidance of one of the largest companies measured by market capitalization on the New York Stock Exchange (if not the largest) was reflected in the stock price and the perception that people had of GE worldwide.

But on a smaller level, Jack was still a giant. Every time I saw Jack in person, I felt like a million bucks. He has the ability to turn his focus to you in a split second and engage you on a personal level. At that moment there is nobody in the world except the two of you, and he is always able to connect by saying just the right thing.

That may be a God-given gift, but it is also an attitude about people honed by real-life experience. His reputation may be bigger than life, but he learned a long time ago not to hold himself *personally* above others, even if his corporate position might be. For instance, someone once called Jack Welch a punk—right to his face, in front of his friends. He was 12 years old.

It was after he lost his temper during a hockey match, threw all his equipment on the ice, and stormed off into the locker room. That's where he was hunted down and verbally skewered—by his mother. Jack recalls:

> She came into the locker room and grabbed me. She said in front of everyone, "You're a punk. If you don't know how to lose well you shouldn't be playing." That was a mistake which toughened me up, and I was able to take the losses equally. It made me competitive in a more effective, decent way. It controlled my fire.

But it was a different mistake, one many years later, that helped create the corporate manager who turned General Electric into one of the largest, most admired companies in the world.

Jack Welch's Best Mistake, in His Own Words

This was 1963 or 1964. I was managing a little pilot plant operation for GE in Pittsfield, Massachusetts. We were making a new plastic. It was me and a couple of other people running an experiment.

 Anyway, something went wrong and it literally blew the roof right off the factory!

It blew the safety locks off the kettles. And the kettles went up through the factory roof and shattered glass everywhere. Nobody was killed. There were people cut and things like that, but nobody was seriously hurt.

I got a call from Charley Reed, a group executive, a couple of levels above me. He was a PhD from MIT, a very curious, scientific fellow. So he brought me to New York. I thought I was going to get fired. But he sat me down and said, "Let's go through the process."

He used a Socratic method. "You're bubbling oxygen in. Why didn't you have it grounded more carefully?" Could we have done this? Could we have done that? We had to realize we were running oxygen through benzyne. We didn't have it properly grounded. A spark was set off and created this atmosphere. So we had to get the oxygen into the solution in a more effective way.

It was all about solving the problem. It wasn't about beating up Jack. Charley Reed's attitude was, "Let's go back and design it right, and when you feel you've got it designed right, let's go."

 It gave me a big lifelong lesson not to kick somebody when they were down.

As hard as I might be on someone when they're flying high and not doing something right, I don't think I've ever done that.

 And second, it gave me exposure to higher-level people. I probably wouldn't have met this guy for another two years or so, and he turned out to be an incredible guiding force in my career.

I established a relationship with him, but mainly what I learned from him is that the last minute you want to be rough on somebody is when they're down.

In the end, the plastic turned out to be a home-run business. It became a very successful plastic. Since I was the first employee and it was successful, it catapulted my career. But along the way I learned a lot about people by the way Charley Reed handled it.

It taught you something about life that you wouldn't normally expect. I call it "never kicking the cat."

About Jack Welch

Jack Welch is the author, with his wife Suzy Welch, of *Winning*, a #1 *Wall Street Journal* and international best seller. In 2001, he wrote his #1 *New York Times* and also international best-selling autobiography (with John A. Byrne), *Jack: Straight from the Gut.*

From 2005 to 2009, together with his wife Suzy, he wrote a widely read weekly column, "The Welch Way." This column appeared in *BusinessWeek* magazine and was published by the *New York Times* syndicate, appearing in more than 45 major newspapers around the world and reaching more than 8 million readers. He recently launched the Jack Welch Management Institute, a unique online MBA program aimed at giving students around the world at every career level the tools to transform their lives and the organizations of the future.

Jack is the head of Jack Welch, LLC, where he serves as special partner with the private equity firm Clayton, Dubilier & Rice and is an adviser to IAC/InterActive Corp. He speaks to business audiences and students around the world.

Born in Salem, Massachusetts, Jack received his undergraduate degree from the University of Massachusetts and an MS and PhD in chemical engineering from the University of Illinois. He began his career with the General Electric Company in 1960, and in 1981 became GE's eighth chairman and CEO. During his 20+-year tenure as CEO, the company's market capitalization rose from $13 billion to $400 billion. In 2000, he was named "Manager of the Century" by *Fortune* magazine.

You can read about Jack's ideas on his web site, The Welch Way (www .welchway.com).

Chapter 2
JOHN C. BOGLE

Created the world's first stock index mutual fund

In 2004, chosen by *Time* magazine for inclusion in the *Time* 100 list of the world's most important and influential people

Named by *Fortune* magazine as one of the investment industry's four Giants of the 20th Century, 1999

t's not often you hear someone blame themselves for something that went wrong at work. John C. Bogle does not hesitate to explain why he was once fired:

I guess I was just too opportunistic, too callow, too self-confident, and maybe even arrogant. All of which, every one of those characteristics which I have come to detest, I have tried to remove from my character to the maximum extent possible.

A shrinking violet he is not.

If you were a Broadway producer casting for the god of investing, the auditions would stop when you heard the voice of Jack Bogle. His time-tested bass booms with authority based on historical research and experience. Of course he's not a god, but there is no question he is an investing legend, having started the Vanguard Group of index-based funds in the 1970s.

"I'm a very demanding, very opinionated, very strong-minded, and very experienced manager. And I'm very interested in history. I walk around thinking on issues before I make decisions, and there are very few cases where someone asks me, 'Did you think of this?' when I haven't thought of it."

The fact is that Jack Bogle changed the way Americans invest when he started the Vanguard Group and introduced the world's first stock index mutual fund.

"Vanguard, meaning we were leaders of a new trend," Bogle proudly recounts. "It was named after Lord Nelson's battle of the Nile, later called by the *New York Times* 'the naval battle of the millennium.' He ended Napoleon's dreams of an empire there in Egypt. He had a loss of zero British ships and he destroyed the entire French navy."

What made index funds different was that they didn't count on the unpredictable and expensive trading of money managers who tried to beat the stock market or its indexes. History showed that most of them didn't beat the market.

The index funds were designed to mirror the indexes themselves, and to keep administrative costs low in order to closely match index returns. By the 1990s, index funds became the dominant style of investing for tens of millions of Americans. They were outperforming almost all managed funds, and still typically outperform 70 percent of them.

Jack Bogle created the first one, but it came about because of a mistake.

It started in the late 1960s, when he was president of the Wellington Fund, which offered conservatively managed investment services. He and the board of directors decided to merge with another investment counseling firm out of Boston: Thorndike, Doran, Paine and Lewis. Thorndike provided more aggressive money management services that would allow Wellington to expand its product line and become more involved in actively managing money.

The expansion of the company succeeded in bringing in millions more dollars, which were actively and aggressively managed by the money managers who reported to Jack Bogle as the president and CEO of the Wellington Management Company. This was the go-go 1960s, when the stock market was roaring in a post–World War II baby boomer bull market.

But the good times didn't last. By the early 1970s, the stock market was mired in a decline that saw Wellington's assets fall, according to Jack Bogle, by an estimated 70 percent.

Jack Bogle's Best Mistake, in His Own Words

In January of 1974, these guys who had so let our shareholders down ganged up and fired me!

 They had more votes than I did. They had put all their friends on the Wellington Management Company board. I didn't think about politics in those days, I was pretty naive. I was unaware of the lessons of history that I had written about in my Princeton senior thesis on the history of this damned business.

I remained as president of Wellington Fund, but I was banned by the board to get into investment management and distribution. In their version of King Solomon, they gave me the administrative third and gave the other guys the investment, advisory, distribution, and marketing two-thirds.

They had given me the worst third of a loaf, the administrative loaf. Don't get me wrong. Administration is important and done responsibly by very good and capable and dedicated people. But it isn't exactly Miss Excitement.

So I had to get into investment management.

I said to the board, "Look, you're representing the funds' stockholders. We'll control how the funds work." I introduced a belly-up theory. "We'll perform every function without which the fund would go belly-up." You'd go belly-up if you had no financial controls. You'd go belly-up if you couldn't get your price in the paper every day. You'd go belly-up if you couldn't process redemptions and couldn't issue new shares. That's all we did. We were an administrative company.

 The directors said, "Wait a minute—you can't get into investment management! You know what the deal is."

And I said, "Aha! This fund isn't managed!" And so the logjam was broken. Disingenuous? Probably, but in a worthy cause.

They made a tactical mistake. They didn't think I could win back at the craps table what I had lost at the poker table.

Vanguard started operating May 1, 1975. In September, I proposed that we start the world's first index fund.

Why? One, it would get me back into investment management. And two, Vanguard was all about being a low-cost provider in this business. So the index fund is the first, most likely, and most obvious fit. It's where the difference in cost shows up every day and you cannot lose over the long run.

We brought out the world's first index fund in 1976. I think it was 1984 before someone else had one.

Vanguard's market share has risen from 1 percent of industry assets back then to more than 10 percent today. That 10 percentage point increase accounts for very close to $880 billion in assets [$1.3 trillion in U.S. mutual funds as of December 31, 2009].

 My best mistake was my biggest mistake. I got fired, but I lived and I learned. I got fired, and created Vanguard.

About John C. Bogle

John C. Bogle, 80, is founder of the Vanguard Group, Inc., and president of the Bogle Financial Markets Research Center. He created Vanguard in 1974 and served as chairman and chief executive officer until 1996 and senior chairman until 2000. He had been associated with a predecessor company since 1951, serving as its chief executive from 1967 to 1974.

The Vanguard Group is one of the two largest mutual fund organizations in the world. Headquartered in Malvern, Pennsylvania, Vanguard comprises more than 100 mutual funds with current assets totaling about $1 trillion. The Vanguard 500 Index Fund, the largest fund in the group, was founded by Jack Bogle in 1975. It was the first index mutual fund.

Education

Princeton University, magna cum laude in economics, 1951

Blair Academy, cum laude 1947

Honorary Degrees

Georgetown University

Princeton University

Immaculata University

Pennsylvania State University

University of Delaware

University of Rochester

New School University

Susquehanna University

Eastern University

Widener University

Albright College

Drexel University

Books by John Bogle

Bogle on Mutual Funds: New Perspectives for the Intelligent Investor (Irwin, 1993).

Common Sense on Mutual Funds: New Imperatives for the Intelligent Investor (John Wiley & Sons, 1999; Fully Updated 10th Anniversary Edition, 2009).

John Bogle on Investing: The First 50 Years (McGraw-Hill, 2000).

Character Counts: The Creation and Building of The Vanguard Group (McGraw-Hill, 2002).

Battle for the Soul of Capitalism (Yale University Press, 2005).

The Little Book of Indexing: The Only Way to Guarantee Your Fair Share of Stock Market Returns (John Wiley & Sons, 2007).

Enough. True Measures of Money, Business, and Life (John Wiley & Sons, 2009).

Books About John Bogle

John Bogle and the Vanguard Experiment: One Man's Quest to Transform the Mutual Fund Industry, by Robert Slater (Irwin, 1996).

Awards

National Council on Economic Education Visionary Award, 2007.

CFA Society of San Francisco Distinguished Speakers Award, 2007.

Center for Corporate Excellence, Exemplary Leader Award, 2006.

Berkeley Award for Distinguished Contributions to Financial Reporting, 2006.

Chester County Business Hall of Fame Award, 2006.

Outstanding Financial Executive Award from the Financial Management Association International, 2005.

Chapter 3

PETER LYNCH

Managed Fidelity's Magellan Fund from 1977 to 1990

Popularized the theme "Invest in what you know"

Author of *One Up on Wall Street* and *Beating the Street*

From his office in Boston, Peter Lynch plays the role of investment guru to the current group of portfolio managers at Fidelity Investments.

"I guess that's what an old fund manager is—a guru," he laughs.

Well, not just any fund manager. If you had invested $1,000 into Lynch's Fidelity Magellan Fund in 1977, you would have had $28,000 by the time he retired from managing the fund in 1990. Not impressed? Look at it this way: If you had put $100,000 of your individual retirement account (IRA) savings into his fund when he started managing it, 13 years later, without adding another dime, you would have had $2.8 million. How does early retirement sound?

Lynch's returns averaged a remarkable 29.2 percent per year during that period, beating the S&P 500 in all but two years. "I loved it. It was great fun," Lynch says. "I just didn't like the hours. Twenty-four/seven wasn't enough. You could spend 24/7 just looking at insurance companies. There weren't enough hours in the day."

And when you talk to Lynch, you realize he probably puts a lot into a 24-hour day. If the speed at which he talks reflects the speed at which he thinks, there's a lot of brainpower being put into his research. He says, "I have a very small transmission. My gearbox is overdrive and off. And you can't *sort of* run a fund."

Now, as research consultant at Fidelity, he meets regularly with the current fund managers, offering them his down-to-earth advice on how to invest successfully in a financial world that seems almost impossible to negotiate.

The striking thing about Lynch's approach is that he makes it sound so simple:

> You ought to be able to explain what you own to an eight-year-old in two minutes or less [and] why you own this thing. If you don't understand it, you're really going to get in trouble.

And while Wall Street has become peppered with technical analysts who look at charts, and quant fund managers who back-test all kinds of theories by computers looking for an advantage that isn't obvious in the balance sheets, Lynch's approach comes across as refreshingly basic:

"There's a 100 percent correlation between earnings and a stock. These are not lottery tickets. Behind every stock is a company. If the company does well, the stock does well. If the company does poorly, the stock does poorly."

Lynch recalls a time he was called upon to predict the future of Dell's stock—by Michael Dell himself.

"I remember we were at some big meeting seven or eight years ago, and somebody said to Dell, up on the stage, 'What's your stock going to do?' And he said, 'Why don't you ask Lynch?' I was out in the audience. And I said, 'Listen, if you earn a lot more money five years from now it'll be higher, and if you earn less it'll be lower."

He also believes that you should look at the world around you to find opportunities on Wall Street. "Invest in what you know" is his classic but down-to-earth advice. For instance, he bought L'Eggs for his mutual fund because his wife had tried on the stockings and raved about them. And his investment history is full of household names that may not have been household names when he first put money into them: Chili's, Dunkin' Donuts, Stop & Shop, and many others.

"I missed Wal-Mart. If I had spent more time in Arkansas I would have done much better with Wal-Mart, but I never saw the stores," he says. "You've got to know what you own, because as the stock goes down, you can get shaken out in a market correction."

And though he looks for great leadership, he doesn't count on it, which leads to one of his better-known sayings:

"Go for a business that any idiot can run—because sooner or later, any idiot probably is going to run it."

One of his long-held goals is finding a stock that goes up tenfold—a "ten-bagger," as he coined it based on baseball's vernacular for doubles, triples, and home runs (two-, three-, and four-baggers).

But while Lynch is appropriately revered for his stock-picking prowess, he didn't get it right every time.

"Be flexible and have no bias and learn from your mistakes," he says.

It doesn't seem like a track record of 29.2 percent per year would include many mistakes, but even Peter Lynch makes them. Including his *best* one.

Peter Lynch's Best Mistake, in His Own Words

It was 1982 or 1983. I was at a Robinson Humphrey conference in Atlanta, and after it was over I went to see Home Depot. They had gone from four stores to six, and all the stores were in Atlanta. Arthur Blank was the president, and was one of two guys really running it. And I had gone to see maybe four of the six stores.

 I bought some stock, and like an idiot I sold it two years later; then it went up 25-fold after that.

It's great if you're right six times out of 10 times, but you want your winners to off-set your losers. You can be wrong a lot, but if your winners can go up threefold, fivefold, 20-fold, you can have a lot of stocks that you lose 50 percent on. You don't ever want to miss one of these enormous stocks.

And I was there at the creation of this thing, I was really early. But I never stayed in touch, and I did a total brain cramp on it. And it went up probably 50-fold after I sold it.

I made a triple on it, but that was just stupidity. If I had just kept in touch, you know, now there are 20 stores out there, now 40, and now up to 400 with no competition....

They offered customers a good value; they had a good balance sheet, not very cyclical at all—I wouldn't have gotten shaken out at all. It could have been a ten-bagger.

I still try to figure out what was going on in my brain.

There were a lot of winners, like Au Bon Pain Co. Inc., which became Panera Bread Company—it was a huge winner, but I stayed with it—Stop & Shop, Dunkin' Donuts, La Quinta Motor Inn, Taco Bell, and other ones. But this one. . . .

 Warren Buffett called me—I think it was 1989 or 1990. And he said, "I'm doing my annual report and I'd love to use one of your quotes in your book—the one about how 'selling your winners and holding on to your losers is like cutting your flowers and watering your weeds.'" And I said, "Sure, go ahead and use it." And that was the mistake I made. Here I was, cutting the flowers and watering the weeds.

It was a great company: a beautiful balance sheet; great record; huge return. It made money very fast; there was a lot of high morale among employees. And they were in only a few states when I sold it. It's different when you're in every state and a competitor comes along like Lowe's—that's a different story. But that was two decades later.

Q. How would you have "stayed in touch"?

I would have visited one of the stores every six months, or called a couple of Wall Street analysts, or called the company every three months, just kind of to update how they're doing. How are the stores doing? What new markets have you gone into? How are the old stores doing? It's all public information; I just would have been in touch. Nothing technical, but what new departments are you starting, and what departments are weak? Who are you competing against? Until then it was basically mom-and-pop shops out here; there were very few of these large do-it-yourself shops. They really helped the consumer out.

Q. Does it still bother you?

No, but it's an example that if you're right, you want to let your winners run. In your lifetime you get very few stocks that go up tenfold—I call it a ten-bagger. You don't want to miss those. And this was like a 25-bagger, or a 30-bagger. This stock—well, the prior year it was under a dollar. You could buy it in 1983 at 25 cents. So it went from 25 cents to $50.

I learned from that if they're really a superior company, watch and ask: Do they still have that competitive advantage? Do they still beat the mom-and-pops? Do they still have no national competitors? Are their existing stores still growing?

Don't sell it. Keep checking up on it. Don't be stubborn, of course. Just because a stock went up doesn't mean it has to go up more; there has to be a reason for it. This stock went up probably a hundredfold, and their earnings went up a hundredfold.

 Don't sell your winners too soon. But stay in touch. You want to make sure the story's still valid.

About Peter Lynch

Peter Lynch is vice chairman of Fidelity Management & Research Company (FMRCo.)—the investment adviser for Fidelity's family of mutual funds—and an advisory board member of the Fidelity funds. Fidelity Investments is the largest mutual fund company in the United States, the number one provider of workplace retirement savings plans, the largest mutual fund supermarket, a leading online brokerage firm, and one of the largest providers of custody and clearing services to financial professionals. Mr. Lynch was portfolio manager of the Fidelity Magellan Fund, which was the best-performing fund in the world under his leadership from May 1977 to May 1990. When he took over the Magellan Fund, it had $20 million in assets. By the time he retired from the fund, it had grown to over $14 billion in assets and had over a million shareholders. Magellan became the biggest fund in the world in 1983, and it continued to outperform all other funds for the next seven years.

Mr. Lynch joined Fidelity in 1969 as a research analyst and was later named director of research. During his tenure at Fidelity, he has served as a managing director of Fidelity Investments, an executive vice president and director of Fidelity Management & Research Company, and a leader of the growth equity group. His first book was the best seller *One Up on Wall Street*. His second book, *Beating the Street*, remained #1 on the *New York Times* best-seller list for eight weeks. His books have been translated into several languages, including Japanese, Swedish, Korean, German, Spanish, French, Polish, Hebrew, Portuguese, and Vietnamese. In 1995, Mr. Lynch co-authored *Learn to Earn*, a beginner's guide to the basics of investing and business.

Before joining Fidelity, he served as a lieutenant in the U.S. Army for two years.

Born in 1944, Mr. Lynch received a bachelor of science degree from Boston College in 1965 and an MBA from the Wharton School at the University of Pennsylvania in 1968. In 1994, he was named Outstanding Alumnus by the

Wharton School. He is a fellow with the American Academy of Arts and Sciences and a member and former director of the Boston Society of Security Analysts.

Mr. Lynch is actively involved with a large number of civic and not-for-profit organizations. He has been recognized with several awards for his efforts, including the National Catholic Education Association 1992 Seton Award, the Massachusetts Society for the Prevention of Cruelty to Children 1993 Family Award, and the 1997 United Way Bay Leadership Award. This year marks his twentieth year as chairman of the Inner City Scholarship Fund, for which he has helped raise over $70 million in partial scholarships for children living in the inner city of Boston and attending Catholic schools.

Mr. Lynch is also the recipient of many professional awards. He was recognized in the Business Hall of Fame of both *Fortune* magazine and the television show *Wall Street Week*.

Chapter 4

BILL GROSS

Co-founder of Pacific Investment Management Company (PIMCO)

Manages PIMCO Total Return Fund, the largest bond fund in the world

Selected, with PIMCO team, as the Morningstar "Fixed-Income Manager of the Year" (2007, 2000, 1998)

The average person doesn't know much about bonds. They represent the conservative part of your retirement savings, IOUs that agree to pay you a certain percentage over time. Useful, maybe, but boring.

But Bill Gross is not your average person. To him, bonds are as exciting and intricate as gambling at the blackjack table in Las Vegas, which at one point in his life he did for 16 hours a day. The lessons he learned there, trying to beat the house and the system stacked against him, taught him how to manage the largest bond fund in the world, PIMCO's Total Return Fund. He says:

> Playing blackjack gave me a sense of risk and reward which I carry with me even today.

Boring bonds and glitzy Las Vegas, linked? You bet. (Sorry.)

It's part of Bill Gross's education as a person and as a money manager.

The co-founder of PIMCO started modestly. He was born in Middletown, Ohio, and graduated from Duke University with a degree in psychology before going into the Navy in the mid-1960s.

"I got out of the Navy and went to graduate school at UCLA and got my MBA degree and tried to find a job as a portfolio manager for stocks," he recalls. "I was unsuccessful. I couldn't do it. Nobody wanted me.

"But I hooked up with this company called Pacific Mutual, which was just about to start a little subsidiary called PIMCO, which would manage a $5 million mutual fund for their life insurance agents. So there it was." An opportunity.

Now he is the portfolio manager of the Total Return Fund, which has almost $200 billion under management. And that little subsidiary called PIMCO, which he co-founded, now employs more than 1,200 people and manages roughly three-quarters of a trillion dollars. And he personally is on *Forbes*'s list as one of the richest people in the world. And it all started with $50 and a trip to the Bahamas on spring break.

It was there, in Nassau, when he found himself with 50 bucks and "no intention to spend it on anything but beer and the ladies," he chuckles. But there were some casinos in town, and after a few beers he sat down at the blackjack table.

"It seemed relatively simple and probably something where I could double my money in about five minutes."

Well, that's not exactly what happened. But it was perhaps his first concrete step toward becoming a billionaire.

Bill Gross's Best Mistake, in His Own Words

I sat down for maybe five minutes, and five minutes later my 50 bucks was gone. I was penniless and begging for beers from my buddies and it was killing my chance for success with the ladies.

I came back to Duke and got into an automobile accident where part of my scalp was damaged. I was in the hospital for plastic surgery for most of the second semester of my senior year.

It turned out the hospital bookstore had a book called *Beat the Dealer*, by Ed Thorp, the originator of blackjack card counting, providing a way to win at the tables.

Remembering my 50 bucks, and having the time recuperating from operations, I read the book and, with a deck of cards, for months I learned the system. I played thousands of hands between myself and the fake dealer, counting the cards and making certain bets that the book suggested.

By the time I graduated, at least in terms of the game, I was making money. So I had about four months between the time I graduated [in 1965] and when I had to report to the Navy—I had signed up to become a Navy pilot to avoid the draft. So I had four months of free time to do nothing.

I took $200, which was all I had left from college of the money that my parents had, thankfully, provided me. So I hopped a freight train to Las Vegas from North Carolina.

I finally reached Vegas with 200 bucks and for the next four months I played blackjack for seven days a week and 16 hours a day. No friends—I mean, who would accompany me on such a trip? Not even a girlfriend. And I stayed in a $6-a-day hotel and got up and played blackjack, and 16 hours later went back to bed and did it all over again.

 The outcome [playing blackjack] was I turned my 200 bucks into $10,000! That sounds impressive, but after I computed the dollars an hour it turned out to be $5 an hour, which puts it all in perspective. But the point is that I won, that I had mastered the game, the system, and put the probabilities in my favor, as opposed to what had happened in Nassau, where I knew nothing and lost my stake within minutes.

The Nassau experience, as far as it being a mistake, and the Vegas experience, as far as it being a success, then led me to wonder—I was going into the Navy and I had three years to contemplate this—what I could do when I got out to employ the same kind of techniques: mathematical prowess, probability, calculations, measured risk taking, in the spirit of trying to win money and take it from somebody else.

Although I had been a psychology major at Duke, what I really wanted to do when I got out of the Navy was to be an investment manager and manage mutual funds, which at the time meant stocks because bonds hadn't even been in anybody's psyche at the time.

When I got out of the Navy I was going to be a portfolio manager, a mutual fund manager, and this was exactly the technique I could use to be a success.

 So my original mistake, my Nassau blackjack experience, led to Las Vegas, which led to graduate school, which led to my taking a job at Pacific Mutual, which led to PIMCO, which then led to the bond market developing in the early

1970s—bonds began to be traded, and I was right there, in the right place at the right time.

Pacific Mutual was a life insurance company and it was pretty small, and it had a lot more bonds than stocks, so I started PIMCO in the direction of bond management, and the rest is my history.

Q. Why did it bug you so much when you lost the $50 in five minutes at the blackjack table?

Because I hate to lose. And I hate to lose stupidly. I knew I should have known better and I could have done better.

 When I got that book, I thought if this book is true, I'm going to beat the system as opposed to having the system beat me.

Q. But how does counting cards in blackjack translate to managing money?

Almost perfectly. The book was based on a calculation called the Kelly system, which was actually a forerunner of the Black-Scholes option methodology that came to dominate the 1970s and the 1980s and gave them [Robert Merton and Myron Scholes] the Nobel Prize.

The Thorp system was a theory of risk management. The Kelly calculation was a crude form of option theory. At UCLA for my graduate degree, I did my master's thesis on the Kelly risk methodology, which I applied to convertible bonds versus stock risk arbitrage. So I learned the fundamentals of risk relative to reward. So when I got money to manage in the bond market, I had a pretty strong fundamental base of knowing how much money I could invest in a particular sector or company and how much risk I could take in the portfolio.

It gave me a sense of risk and reward that I carry with me even until today.

And if you're going to do something, make sure you understand not only the rules but the probabilities of winning or losing, which I knew nothing about.

About Bill Gross

Bill Gross is a founder of PIMCO, managing director and co-CIO in the Newport Beach office. He has been associated with PIMCO for more than 38 years and oversees the management of more than $800 billion of fixed-income securities. He is the author of numerous articles on the bond market, as well as the book *Everything You've Heard about Investing Is Wrong*, published in 1997. He appears frequently in national publications and media. Among the awards he has received, Morningstar named Mr. Gross and his investment team Fixed-Income Manager of the Year for 1998, 2000, and 2007, making him the first person to receive this award more than once. Morningstar stated that he demonstrated "excellent investment skill, the courage to differ from consensus, and the commitment to shareholders necessary to deliver outstanding long-term performance." In 2000, Mr. Gross received the Bond Market Association's Distinguished Service Award. In 1996, he became the first portfolio manager inducted into the Fixed Income Analysts Society's Hall of Fame for his major contributions to the advancement of fixed-income analysis and portfolio management. In a survey conducted by *Pensions & Investments* magazine in 1993, Mr. Gross was recognized by his peers as the most influential authority on the bond market in the United States. He holds an MBA from the Anderson School of Management at the University of California, Los Angeles. He received his undergraduate degree from Duke University.

Chapter 5
WILLIAM O'NEIL

Founder of *Investor's Business Daily* (*IBD*)

Inventor of CAN SLIM stock investing strategy

Youngest person (at the time) to buy a seat on the New York Stock Exchange (NYSE)

UCLA's legendary basketball coach John Wooden used to start the first practice of the season instructing his players on how to put on their shoes and socks.

William O'Neil, the famed investor and founder of *Investor's Business Daily*, loves that kind of focus. "He was trying to eliminate every possible controllable item that could beat them."

It wasn't just the practical guidance so that players could avoid blisters or a shoe coming untied and forcing the player out of the game. O'Neil saw it as a lesson for anybody trying to succeed. "Wooden said the difference between a champion and almost a champion was paying attention to every little detail."

Detail. While nobody can match Wooden's record as a college basketball coach, neither can many businesspeople match William O'Neil's investing career for creativity, performance, and impact.

Or his own attention to detail.

When he was a kid growing up in Texas, he used to go down to South Padre Island—even then an entrepreneur at heart—and sell sandwiches. He recalls, "I learned that sandwiches got soggy near seawater."

Detail. It's why his company, William O'Neil + Company, has amassed an enormous database of information on stocks going back to the 1880s. "We've learned that there's really not that much that has changed. The chart patterns in 1910, 1930, and 1950 are the same as they are now," he says. "The only difference is that back in those old days it was J. P. Morgan and Edward Harriman and these pools that would be running stocks up, and since the 1930s it's been the better mutual funds that have been the dominant factor in the market in determining what these stocks will do. But the patterns are really the same."

Detail. It is the reason that he founded the financial daily newspaper *Investor's Business Daily* (originally *Investor's Daily*) in 1984. "I'd be traveling around and I'd pick up the *Wall Street Journal* and there was nothing in it of the sort of data we needed, the things that we knew were important. They were taking the old AP [Associated Press] tables and slapping them in."

But Bill O'Neil went further than simply collecting or publishing detail. He interpreted it.

"We now have stock winning models from 1880 through to today, and we looked at all the variables, the fundamentals—earnings, return on equity, and products—and then we looked at all the technical things. And ours is a combination of all these different variables: sponsorship, industry conditions, products. And we have a set of rules, a profile of what a leading stock looks like.

"It's not perfect," he allows. "We make our mistakes, but we have rules that if you make a mistake, you cut it and go on to the next thing."

In fact, O'Neil came up with a trading strategy based on all that data, known by the acronym CAN SLIM. The strategy starts with the following information.

C: Current earnings

A: Annual earnings

N: New product or service?

S: Supply and demand (based on volume)

L: Leader or laggard?

I: Institutional ownership

M: Major market indexes and their trends

This information is then compared to the performance of thousands of successful stocks based on years of research—and O'Neil's own trading experience.

"Our rule number one is that with every single stock you buy, when it goes down 7 or 8 percent below what you've paid for it, it has to go out. No exceptions. And the reason for it is maybe half the time it might turn around and go up, but the other half of the time it rolls over and can go down 70 percent. And if you sit with it, that's how people get hurt."

O'Neil learned something early on in his "buy low, sell high" investing career. "What was very eye-opening was that it actually was 'buy high, sell higher' based on research proving you had to buy quality, higher-priced stocks, rather than bargain-basement ones in the old 'buy low, sell high' philosophy," he notes. Buying the stock was only half of the equation. You had to get the other part right, too, and O'Neil says:

No one has any idea when you should sell a stock.

"We've done studies on when outstanding stocks topped, and we've learned some rules that force us into saying you've got to do it this way. And one of our rules is that when a market leader finally tops, the average correction is 72 percent. You're a long, long time coming back—just to break even."

O'Neil gives workshops on applying the rules of the CAN SLIM strategy in the real world. The American Association of Individual Investors hails the approach as the number one strategy out of over 50 widely known investing methods from January 1998 through December 31, 2009.

The success of CAN SLIM is part of the reason why *Investor's Business Daily* survives during an era in which newspapers are shutting down across the country. Only 20 to 25 percent of *IBD*'s revenue comes from advertising. The rest comes from subscribers and workshops that are given to educate CAN SLIM followers on the stock-picking strategy.

One of the more interesting aspects of talking with William O'Neil is the feeling you get that, in his eyes, picking stocks and reading *Investor's Business Daily* are more than a strategy for succeeding in investing—they're part of an organized approach to succeeding in life itself. How many other newspapers publish "Secrets to Success"?

IBD's 10 Secrets to Success

Investor's Business Daily has spent years analyzing leaders and successful people in all walks of life. Most have 10 traits that, when combined, can turn dreams into reality. "Each day, we highlight one," says O'Neil.

1. **HOW YOU THINK IS EVERYTHING:** Always be positive. Think success, not failure. Beware of a negative environment.
2. **DECIDE UPON YOUR TRUE DREAMS AND GOALS:** Write down your specific goals and develop a plan to reach them.
3. **TAKE ACTION:** Goals are nothing without action. Don't be afraid to get started. Just do it.
4. **NEVER STOP LEARNING:** Go back to school or read books. Get training and acquire skills.
5. **BE PERSISTENT AND WORK HARD:** Success is a marathon, not a sprint. Never give up.
6. **LEARN TO ANALYZE DETAILS:** Get all the facts, all the input. Learn from your mistakes.
7. **FOCUS YOUR TIME AND MONEY:** Don't let other people or things distract you.
8. **DON'T BE AFRAID TO INNOVATE; BE DIFFERENT:** Following the herd is a sure way to mediocrity.
9. **DEAL AND COMMUNICATE WITH PEOPLE EFFECTIVELY:** No person is an island. Learn to understand and motivate others.
10. **BE HONEST AND DEPENDABLE; TAKE RESPONSIBILITY:** Otherwise, Nos. 1–9 won't matter.

It is perhaps because of O'Neil's focus on success in stocks *and* in life that he doesn't just dwell on the detail of data gathered from the past. He can also look forward. And he does so with hope, no matter what the market conditions are. He explains:

We had 26 stock market cycles. And every single cycle was led by innovators, entrepreneurs, and new inventions: railroads, airplane, radio, automobile, automatic elevator . . .

"Today it's the Internet and semiconductors, and there will be more exciting growth areas in the future. Technology is so strong; the freedom, the opportunity is out there all the time, no matter who's in Washington. There's an Apple out there somewhere.

"Each cycle brings on sectors, with technology and innovation. The Internet is still a young baby. That's what drives the American economy.

"And the Chinese saw the Soviet Union imploding, and saw that Americans were making money, so China is copying us; they're copying our model because they saw the communist system is not that productive."

If you look at *IBD*'s "Secrets to Success," there's one secret that is especially relevant to this book. It is number 6, "Learn to analyze details: Get all the facts, all the input. Learn from your mistakes."

O'Neil applied that in a way that launched the rest of his career. He began as a stockbroker in 1958 and came up with rules to buy the right stocks at the right time. By 1961 he was pretty good at picking winners. He bought a seat on the New York Stock Exchange (at age 30) in 1963 and founded William O'Neil + Company, which developed the first computerized daily securities database, and currently tracks over 200 data items for over 10,000 companies.

But his achievements might never have reached the level they are at today without the time he made his best mistake.

William O'Neil's Best Mistake, in His Own Words

I was starting to use charts, and I bought Brunswick and Great Western Financial and AMF. . . . All of these were leaders in the early 1960s. I bought them at the right time in the right way and I had some very good positions and profits.

 But when the stocks topped, I held on to them too long and I gave up all that gain.

I was so upset for blowing it and having nothing to show for it because I'd been dead right in the right stocks at the right time, and here I gave it all back.

So what I did was I spent several months analyzing in detail every single stock I bought in the prior year. I had a red pen, and I marked on charts where I bought and where

I sold, and I had a big accounting worksheet where I posted day by day what these stocks did all the way up—the prices, the volume changes—and really went into a lot of detail.

 And it's amazing, but it finally dawned on me, something that should have been obvious: that I had finally figured out how to buy the stocks, the real leaders, but I had no plan on when to sell.

I had never thought about it. That's when I developed sell rules, on when to sell stocks on the way up when certain things happen. And I found out also that all these stocks topped when the market topped. So I figured out you had to have buy and sell rules on general market activity also.

And I developed those rules, finalizing a system that worked and made some sense. Before, I only had half of the ballgame. I had offense but no defense.

 It's like a tennis player who has a forehand and doesn't know how to hit a backhand.

There was one other thing that showed up in this. One stock that I really botched up was Certainteed. It had taken off and then had a sharp correction and I was taken out with about a two-point profit, and the stock turned around and doubled or tripled. So I studied that particularly well and wrote out new rules so that if I got into a situation like that again I could handle it correctly.

And that was a rule I came up with that if you buy a stock coming out of a base, and it goes up 20 percent in only three weeks or less, then you must hold it for another five weeks and then reevaluate. That kind of action is so exceptional that no matter what's going on you've got to give it more latitude and room.

That helped immensely a year later when Syntex, the first company with the oral contraceptive pill, came along. This stock takes off and runs up just like Certainteed—a specific percentage in a certain time—and I put it in this automatic rule where I have to hold it for X amount of time, and survived through a sharp correction. It became the big winner of the year. It went up to $550 from $100 in six months.

This was the first time that I put everything together right. I bought the right stock at the right time, didn't get shaken out, held it right, and sold it right.

 The key here is that I had very specific rules. If I had been doing what I was doing a couple of years earlier, I would have sold this stock much, much earlier because it went through two sharp corrections.

So fouling up like that, and being forced to sit down and see what dumb things I did that time showed a couple of glaring weaknesses I had. I had buy rules, but I had no way to handle that Certainteed situation.

[O'Neil developed his rules because he found that almost everything about investing in stocks is contrary to human nature. Even a highly educated person will do the wrong thing after buying a stock. "If he buys it at 50 and it goes to 40, he won't sell it. The math and psychology fool most people." Simply put, O'Neil developed rules that take the emotion out of investing.]

 You've got to have rules rather than just going by how you feel. Because if you go by how you feel, you're scared or hoping all the time.

About William O'Neil

Born in Oklahoma and raised in Texas, William J. (Bill) O'Neil made his first investment of only $300 in Procter & Gamble while serving in the Air Force in his 20s. Then he joined Hayden Stone as a stockbroker, and began his landmark studies of the greatest stock market winners to determine the specific traits they had in common. After a 20-fold increase in his own account in 26 months, Bill O'Neil bought a seat on the New York Stock Exchange at age 30, the youngest person at that time to do so, and formed William O'Neil + Company, one of the most highly respected securities research firms in the United States. He was the first to computerize daily stock information in the 1960s, which led him to develop a strategy for identifying those traits, called the CAN SLIM investing strategy. Today, the CAN SLIM method is the leading growth strategy and outperformed the S&P 500 in good markets and bad.*

With the launch of *Investor's Business Daily* (*IBD*) in 1984, Mr. O'Neil opened the playing field to everyday investors. *IBD*'s unique screening tools provide a fast track to CAN SLIM stocks, and the educational support from seminars and *IBD* University have helped build a rare story of investing success for many individuals, particularly in the current economic climate. Bill O'Neil is the recipient of numerous awards and the author of several best-selling

---

*The American Association of Individual Investors' independent real-time study found that *IBD*'s CAN SLIM investment system achieved +2,763 percent over 12 years, an average of 35.3 percent a year versus 3.3 percent for the S&P 500 (1998 through 2009, AAII Stock Screen).

books, including the classic *How to Make Money in Stocks: A Winning System in Good Times or Bad*, long considered must reading by leading market thinkers, historians, financial professionals, and economists alike. The recently updated fourth edition of the book covers the 2008–2009 bear market and includes 100 charts of winning stocks that reveal common patterns all stocks share before they make big moves up in price. His other best-selling books include *The Successful Investor*, *24 Essential Lessons to Investing Success*, and *How to Make Money Selling Stocks Short*. He is the editor of numerous books, including the *Leaders & Success* book series.

Chapter 6
JIM ROGERS

Co-founded the Quantum Fund

Visiting professor at Columbia University

Has traveled around the world—on a motorcycle!

J im Rogers is somebody who makes good use of time. He's the only person who worked out in the gym even as I interviewed him. I'm not sure whether he was on the treadmill or the exercise bike, but when a guy is panting into my ear on the phone, I don't tend to ask a lot of questions. (Drive home safely, I'll be here all week.) The thing is, at the end of the interview Jim was probably in better shape than I was and already a whole lot richer. Maybe that's because he knows how to use his time.

As a successful fund manager, Jim hasn't wasted time. He has tended to position himself before others figure out what he already knows. "I don't usually invest in something that everybody else is investing in," he says.

I find something very cheap, where positive changes are taking place, and I buy it.

Like when he began a commodities fund in August of 1998. That fund began in an era when most investors were focused on finding the next dot-com stock. We all know what happened to those.

"For the first four or five months," he recalls, "the fund went down. There was the Asian crisis, and a few other things. But starting in January of 1999, the commodities bull market began. But even then it took several years before most people even knew commodities were going up, and very few people to this day have invested in commodities even though they've been the best part of the market for over 10 years."

But don't call him a contrarian. It's too simplistic. There's a lot more thought put into his investments than just going against the grain:

I don't buy something just to be contrary. I buy because I think there's a reason. And the things that are cheap are the things that nobody's looking at. And the things that are extremely expensive—that I can sell or sell short—are the things that everybody is looking at. And normally when everybody owns something, there's nobody left to buy it. And when there are negative changes taking place, it's time to sell.

Jim has a good reason to believe that there is still room for commodities prices to go higher. He recalls a conference in Prague. "The guy speaking at one point asked the audience how many had ever owned gold. Seventy-six percent of the people in that room—successful investors—had never owned gold in their lives. And that's gold. I know if he had asked about soybeans or something like that it would be nobody except me who could have said yes."

Jim goes against the established trends in fashion as well. Anybody who has seen him on CNBC, Bloomberg, or Fox will identify him by his bow tie. But in that case he's not expecting everyone else to go along. He says bow ties are much more practical. "They're cheaper than long ties," he says. "And you can't get them dirty. You don't spill soup on them."

His commitment to commodities is not a fleeting one. "My main investments now are commodities because the fundamentals are improving. But the supply of all commodities continues to be under duress. So if the world economy improves, commodities are going to be a great place to be because of the shortages developing. If the world economy does not improve, commodities are still a good place to be because governments are printing money. And throughout history, when people have printed money, it's led to higher prices. This is the first time in recorded history that nearly everybody is printing money. And by the way, if they don't get better they're going to print even more money, which is going to be even better for commodities. We have all learned that in times of printing money, real assets are the way to protect yourselves, and you make money.

"So to me, it doesn't matter what happens to the economy; commodities are going to do well either way."

And while many other investors who like commodities point to China as the driving force, Jim doesn't join that bandwagon.

"The Chinese economy is one-tenth the size of the economy of America and Europe," he points out, "so whatever China's doing they can't be a major factor in any market. Sure, they're buying and they're doing well and they're growing, but Europe and America are 10 times the size of the Chinese economy. It's coming from everywhere. So sure, China's part of it. But Asia's part of it; everybody's part of it."

Jim Rogers's Best Mistake, in His Own Words

I was fairly new in the business. To be exact, it was January of 1970. I came to the conclusion that we were going to have a bear market. We had been in a bear market, and it was going to get a lot worse. It was rather radical thinking at the time.

So I took what little money I had and bought puts. All my money was in puts. By May, I had tripled my money. It was at a time that firms that had been around a hundred years were going out of business. I mean, it was the worst bear market since 1938—it was a doozy.

There I was—I had tripled my money. And on the day the market hit bottom, I sold my puts and I had tripled my money. And I said, "Boy, this is easy."

So I took my profits, I waited for the market to rally, and it did; two months later I took all my money and sold six companies short—I didn't want to buy puts because puts were the big thing by then. Within two months of that, I was wiped out. I didn't have any staying power and the market kept rallying.

What I learned from that of course is how little I knew about markets, and how little I knew about what *could* happen in markets. And interestingly enough, all six of those companies eventually went bankrupt. In fact, within five years they were all bankrupt. That does not mean I didn't lose everything first. I did, because I didn't understand markets well enough as far as trading went, or anything else.

It made me realize that if I were going to take a position I always assumed that everybody knew what I knew. I now know that the efficient market theory is garbage.

[*Note:* The efficient market hypothesis (EMH), according to Businessdictionary.com, asserts that the price of a financial instrument reflects all the information currently available on it, and that the price will instantly change to reflect new information.]

Some people are better than others at looking ahead, but I had always assumed that everybody knew that XYZ was a garbage company and would collapse. But they didn't!

 What I've learned is that it takes a while for people to figure out what's happening, or what's really happening, and in the interim there are going to be market moves that people don't understand because they don't understand the deeper reality. So I now have to figure out a way to allow for the fact that other people don't understand totally what's going on.

So that was probably my worst mistake on a percentage basis. And when I speak to students I say that it's a good thing to lose everything once or twice—we all know stories of people who failed at something and then came back—but do it when you're young. Do it when it's five thousand and not five million.

About Jim Rogers

Jim Rogers, a native of Demopolis, Alabama, is an author, financial commentator, and successful international investor. He has been frequently featured in *Time*, the *Washington Post*, the *New York Times*, *Barron's*, *Forbes*, *Fortune*, the *Wall Street Journal*, the *Financial Times*, the *Business Times*, the *Straits Times*, and many other media outlets worldwide. He has also appeared as a regular commentator and columnist in various media and has been a visiting professor at Columbia University.

After attending Yale University and Oxford University, Rogers co-founded the Quantum Fund, a global investment partnership. During the next 10 years, the portfolio gained 4,200 percent, while the S&P 500 rose less than 50 percent. Rogers then decided to retire—at age 37. Continuing to manage his own portfolio, he kept busy serving as a professor of finance at the Columbia University Graduate School of Business, and, in 1989 and 1990, as the moderator of WCBS's *The Dreyfus Roundtable* and FNN's *The Profit Motive with Jim Rogers*.

In 1990–1992, Rogers fulfilled his lifelong dream: motorcycling 100,000 miles across six continents, a feat that landed him in the *Guinness Book of World Records*. As a private investor, he constantly analyzed the countries through which he traveled for investment ideas. He chronicled his one-of-a-kind journey in *Investment Biker: On the Road with Jim Rogers*. Jim also embarked on a Millennium Adventure. He traveled for 1,101 days on his round-the-world, Guinness World Record journey. Passing through 116 countries, he covered more than 245,000 kilometers, which he recounted in his book *Adventure Capitalist: The Ultimate Road Trip*. Another book he wrote, *Hot Commodities: How Anyone Can Invest Profitably in the World's Best Market*, was published in 2004. His recent book *A Bull in China* describes his experiences in China as well as the changes and opportunities there. His latest book is *A Gift to My Children*.

Chapter 7

MOHAMED EL-ERIAN

Co-CIO and co-CEO of PIMCO

Former president of Harvard Management Company

Member of the National Bureau of Economic Research

Mohamed El-Erian doesn't want to be surrounded by yes-men. (Or yes-women for that matter.) He likes to come out of business meetings and ask his colleagues, "What should we have done differently in that meeting?"

He does it because he believes that by asking the right questions you can learn from mistakes. "No one goes through life without making mistakes," he says, adding:

Life is too unpredictable and we are too imperfect of instruments to deal with life. So we will make inadvertent mistakes. The important thing is not to make the same mistakes over and over again.

That willingness to question virtually everything is well suited to PIMCO, where he serves as co-CIO and co-CEO with Bill Gross. "That's why the fit is so wonderful," he says, "because I've ended up at a firm that has a process that is doing exactly what I learned when I was 17 years old, which is always to try to question and think about issues from different perspectives."

His diplomat father—who once worked at the United Nations—was a good role model. "While we were living in Paris we used to get four different newspapers," El-Erian recalls.

"So I asked my dad why we needed four different newspapers, and he said, 'Because you've got to view things from different perspectives.' My dad would say: 'Don't become hostage to one way of seeing things.'"

El-Erian is used to seeing things from outside the mainstream. He was born in New York, but spent his early years in his father's home in Egypt. At age 10 the family moved back to New York, where he rooted for the Miracle Mets in a town in love with the Yankees. Then he moved with his family to Paris, where he learned French. Because he was moving around so much as a young man, he actually asked his parents to let him attend boarding school in England because he wanted to stay in one place while going to school. And he now lives in the quintessential California town of Newport Beach, but he speaks not only English and French, but Arabic, not exactly a common local dialect.

The practice of looking at things from different perspectives is not just an intriguing theory at PIMCO. It's actually part of the decision-making process.

"At least once a year we take time to step back, not just from the markets but from ourselves," El-Erian says, "and we invite fore-thinkers to come and share with us their views in the fields they have chosen, because they have outside-the-box views. These tend to be authors and future policy makers—Ben Bernanke came at one point. We let the other people to tell us how we should be thinking about the world. We debate these things on their ground."

Another thing PIMCO does is to take its brand-new MBAs, get them up on the stage, and ask them to tell their colleagues what they think of the world—as opposed to having senior people tell them what *they* think of the world.

"We also have a shadow investment committee," El-Erian says. "And the shadow investment committee's role is to question the investment committee. The representative of the shadow committee sits on the investment committee, and he's judged ultimately on the extent to which he has acted as a catalyst for the shadow committee to question what the investment committee comes up with."

And there have been concrete investment ideas from the PIMCO process. For example, back in 1999, they invited a Chinese speaker who got them to think very seriously about the way China was evolving, and the extent to which it was achieving critical mass in terms of its development process. And very early on PIMCO started bringing China into the equation to explain what was going on. El-Erian recalls, "We wouldn't have done that had we not gotten someone who lives this stuff to signal to us, 'Hey, you guys should be looking at this seriously,' because China wasn't on the radar screen of the U.S. investor at all.

"We also invited a professor who studies successful firms who helped us think about why it is historically that successful firms have not handled paradigm changes easily."

What is it that made IBM respond to the PC revolution by creating a better mainframe? What is it that made the top four tire companies in the United States respond to Michelin's introduction of the radial tire by going from three-ply to five-ply tires?

Why is it that successful companies, with a tremendous amount of capital and R&D, see the changes coming—because IBM saw the PC revolution coming and the tire companies saw the radial tire coming—but react in the wrong way and aren't so successful afterward?

Good questions. Mohamed El-Erian has a lot of them.

Mohamed El-Erian's Best Mistake, in His Own Words

When I was in high school in England, I applied for Cambridge University. I had a very good economics teacher. He gave me a book that had just come out, and he told me, "You must read this book. And whatever happens, you must bring it up in your interview because it will show the professors that you really are interested in economics and in all things—news, et cetera."

And I read that book, basically digested it, prepared my little speech, and off I went for my interview.

The interview was in a room with two professors, one doing all the questioning, and one taking notes. We were going all over the place, and I looked at my watch, and

I knew the interview would last one hour, and it had been 55 minutes and I hadn't mentioned the book.

So I was being asked about some subject, and completely out of the blue I said, "Oh, this reminds me of this recent book I read which I found very interesting." Of course there was no linkage at all. The fellow taking notes put down his notepad and said, "Really? Tell me about it."

Off I went with great enthusiasm with this well-prepared monologue about this book. And he got up, went to his bookcase, pulled out one of them, and sat down with it. Then he asked me a very simple question that basically demolished the whole argument of the book I was discussing.

And I was struggling to give an answer, and I couldn't give an answer, and then he flipped over to me his off-print, which was a critique of the book that he had just published in one of the journals, and he said to me,

 "Mohamed, you should not believe everything you read. Just because it's printed doesn't make it right."

I walked out of that interview completely deflated. It was my dream to go to Cambridge. And it never occurred to me that a book that I had read that had been published could not be right. I was absolutely devastated because it was a completely self-inflicted mistake.

But for a 17-year-old, who had great faith in anything that was printed, that was a very important lesson that I should question lots and lots of things.

 And if you look at my big investment calls, they were all about questioning things.

Let me give you an example. Early on, like many other people, we (at PIMCO) identified that Argentina was going to have problems. It wasn't a difficult call, because we had evidence every single day that the country wasn't acting well. This was in 2000, and they defaulted in December of 2001.

I remember sitting on panels where the first question would be, "How do you feel about Argentina?" and the response would be firmly in the negative. And then people would ask, "How are you positioned?" And I would say, "We are underweight Argentina." And then the next question would come, "How underweight are you?"

At the time, Argentina was over 20 percent of the emerging market index. So you would get somebody to say, "I am very underweight; I only hold 15 percent." Another one would say, "I'm very underweight; I only hold 17 percent." Then they would come to us [PIMCO], and we would say, "We don't have any." And people would say, "What do you mean you don't have any? It's 20 percent of the index!" They would say, "Your portfolio doesn't behave as if you don't own any." And we would smile.

What PIMCO did at the time was to question this notion that you should hold a credit simply because it's in the index [the JPMorgan Emerging Market Bond Index]. Our thinking was, well, if we believe this country is going face all this difficulty, it's irresponsible to hold 15 percent in that index.

So what did we do? We did something very simple. We went out and looked at countries that were highly correlated to Argentina because they shared regional character-istics. We said, "Let's hold no Argentina, but let's hold a little bit more of these other countries. If Argentina goes down, we're fully protected, and if Argentina goes up, we'll catch some of the upside." Before Argentina went down, that index was behaving as if we owned Argentina. And when it went down—Argentina collapsed 65 percent—the index ended up being down 1 percent, and we were up over 20 percent!

 The PIMCO process is to always question. Don't take on risk simply because other people are taking on risk.

About Mohamed El-Erian

Mohamed El-Erian is a co-CEO and co-CIO of PIMCO, based in Newport Beach, California. He rejoined PIMCO in 2008 after serving for two years as president and CEO of Harvard Management Company, the entity that manages Harvard's endowment and related accounts. Dr. El-Erian also served as a member of the faculty of Harvard Business School and as deputy treasurer of the uni-versity. He first joined PIMCO in 1999 as managing director and was a senior member of PIMCO's portfolio management and investment strategy group. Before coming to PIMCO, Dr. El-Erian was a managing director at Salomon Smith Barney/Citigroup in London, and before that, he spent 15 years at the International Monetary Fund (IMF) in Washington, D.C. Dr. El-Erian has pub-lished widely on international economic and finance topics and has served on several boards and committees, including the Emerging Markets Traders Association and the IMF's Committee of Eminent Persons. He is also a mem-ber of the U.S. Treasury Borrowing Advisory Committee and the IMF's Capital Markets Consultative Group, and chairs Microsoft's Investment Advisory Committee. He has 25 years of investment experience and holds a PhD in economics from Oxford University. He received his undergraduate degree from Cambridge University.

Chapter 8

ROBERT PRECHTER

Founder and president of Elliott Wave International

Chosen "Guru of the Decade" (1980s) by Financial News Network (now CNBC)

Author or editor of 13 books, including *New York Times* best seller *Conquer the Crash*

For the rest of Robert Prechter's life, he will always be linked to something he did in 1987:

Prechter . . . known for his prediction of the 1987 stock market crash . . . (*Wall Street Journal*)

Prechter . . . [who] forecast the 1987 market crash . . . (*New York Times*)

Prechter . . . who told investors to sell their stocks weeks before the October 1987 crash . . . (*Barron's*)

When you're a stock market analyst, it doesn't get much bigger than predicting a crash—and getting it right. But Prechter wants to be appreciated for more than that.

"People tend to say, 'Oh, he just calls crashes,'" Prechter says, "but I was super-bullish through the whole 1980s, actually from 1975 forward."

He wants to be known for his overall predictions.

"If they're going to go back that far," he says, "I wish they'd say I wrote a super-bullish book in 1978 (*Elliott Wave Principle—Key to Market Behavior*), updated it in 1982, and called for a great bull market that would turn into a great mania, which ultimately fully retraced."

Fully retraced?

That's part of the lexicon of the man known for popularizing key theories of the Elliott Wave Principle (EWP). It was a set of theories first put forth in the 1930s by Ralph Nelson Elliott, who argued that people are rhythmical beings who go through certain waves of behavior. Those mass psychological waves affect the financial markets, Elliott said, and if you look at the history of the stock market you would see repeated patterns that were directed by that investor psychology. When people were optimistic about an investment, they bid the price up; when they were pessimistic about it, they bid the price down.

Prechter found the theories of EWP engaging. Perhaps it is not a coincidence that he graduated from Yale not with a degree in business or finance, but in psychology.

"I think that waves of social mood are causal to the market's movements," he says. "They are also causal to all social action, and they're the engine of history. So fundamentals lag and follow waves of social mood. They are the result."

Put another way, the fundamentals of corporations and the economy— such as earnings and gross domestic product (GDP) growth—do not cause the rise or fall of prices on Wall Street. Social behavior within a market does. That's why Prechter, as a technical analyst, watches the wave movements of a market more than he watches the fundamentals of the economy.

"Fundamental analysis is information from outside the marketplace," Prechter says. "For instance, let's say the company's earnings are 'x,' and the president's policy is 'y.' And from this information we're going to try to guess where the market is going. The technician is someone who studies information generated by market behavior itself. So he's watching price movement, market psychology, the extent of optimism and pessimism. He's looking at the speed and breadth of the market. He's looking at volume—things that are internal to the market."

It is here that Prechter sees the value of following wave patterns. "Wave patterns include all those things: sentiment, momentum, even volume observations. So it's a 100 percent technical approach."

Prechter first learned about Elliott Wave theory in the early 1970s, shortly after he graduated from college and began working with A. J. Frost. He was reading Richard Russell's *Dow Theory Letters*, and in 1975 came across a copy of Hamilton Bolton's book on the subject. He wanted to know more.

So he went to the library. And he searched for two books written by R. N. Elliott.

"The Library of Congress didn't have them—I checked there first." But he did find them listed in the card catalog of the New York Public Library. "They had both of his books on microfilm. So I paid them a few cents a page and had them print the books out. I spent about two years putting it all together."

Was the information translatable from books written so long ago, in 1938 and 1946?

"Oh, completely!" he says.

That research, and his application of EWP, became the foundation for virtually all of his market analysis since. It began in earnest during his years as a technical analyst for Merrill Lynch in the mid-1970s, where people were only discussing the most basic ideas of how waves are formed.

He took that further, publishing his first *Elliott Wave Theorist* newsletter in 1976. The newsletter has been published continually since 1979. Prechter has gone on to write 13 books, formed Elliott Wave International (which publishes analysis on the financial markets), served as president of the Market Technicians Association, and created a theory of social mood called socionomics, in which he analyzes social trends based on mass psychological waves. To that end he has founded Socionomics International and the non-profit Socionomics Foundation; written the book *Socionomics*; and lectured on the topic at major academic institutions, including MIT and the London School of Economics.

It all started with Elliott, and Prechter's trip to the library.

"Most people," Prechter says, describing the additional data he gathered, "talk about five waves in bull markets, and three waves in bear markets. But Elliott had many more details and reasoning behind it—many more examples and more comments about why he thought this was happening."

His successful application of the theories paid off for him during the 1980s bull market, during which he won awards for market timing. The Financial

News Network, now CNBC, named him the "Guru of the Decade" in 1989. And his predictions on the future of the stock market post-'87 crash were claimed by some to be so powerful as to move the markets (an assertion that Prechter considers ridiculous). In the months after Black Monday in October 1987, subscriptions to Prechter's *Elliott Wave Theorist* surged to some 20,000.

But if there are waves in financial markets, so are there waves in business careers, and Prechter believes he has experienced ups and downs just like those in the stock market: "I've plotted them. I've plotted subscriptions."

He got the equivalent of a bull market third wave by getting the 1980s right, but his predictions in the 1990s did not fare as well. And his consistently bearish tone during the roaring 1990s and into the 2000s created critics who considered his Elliott Wave theory less than legitimate technical analysis. He has frequently predicted stock market collapses, and picked lower levels in the major indexes that the stock market didn't remotely approach.

Here's how Eric Tyson, author of books such as *Personal Finance for Dummies*, puts it: "The underperformance of Prechter's newsletter is nothing short of astonishing and stunning! On an annualized basis [from the beginning of 1985 to the end of May 2009], Prechter has underperformed the broad U.S. stock market Wilshire 5000 index by a whopping 25 percent per year!"

But Prechter defends his performance in a couple of ways. First, he says, "It's a probability game. People in my business are trying to predict the future. And the quality of the predictions has to be considered. I don't think anybody's ever made the prediction of a mania like I did."

And he also points out an improved track record in recent years. Market-Watch stated that the Elliott Wave Financial Forecaster (EWFF) was one of the few to make money during the market collapse in 2008. And in September of 2009, it cited success in the rough markets:

> In fact right now, it looks like pessimism has paid off. Over the past 12 months through July [2009], EWFF is up 11.4 percent by *Hulbert Financial Digest* count, versus negative 20.03 percent for the dividend-reinvested Wilshire 5000 Total Stock Market Index.

> Over the past three years, the letter has achieved an annualized gain of 3.58 percent, against negative 5.78 percent annualized for the total return Wilshire 5000. Over the past 10 years, the letter has achieved a

1.2 percent annualized gain, compared to negative 0.26 percent annualized for the total return Wilshire.

Part of what Prechter got right was the cataclysmic peak of the stock market in 2007. He says it was a classic fifth wave top. And for those who say the peak was reached because of easy money, Prechter agrees. But he says the easy credit was the result of the public mood toward money.

Credit doesn't come from nowhere. It doesn't come from the Fed. It was when we finally got into the fifth wave that the debtors said, "I want to borrow because I'll have no problem paying it back," so they were optimistic. And the creditors said, "We trust these people to pay us back. Even if they're broke, and they want a house, we're willing to finance it." And I think such extreme optimism is almost as if these people weren't thinking.

Prechter looks at the current point of his career as the beginning of a soaring bull stage. "The good news is I've actually got to get a fifth wave and I think things are improving now. I'm deeply in it."

His career is marked by great ups and downs in stock market prognostication, but an element of his experience that is not often examined is his market-forecasting firm, Elliott Wave International. His best mistake, in his mind, happened during the bear phase of his career.

"I was in a wave four," he says, "a long-drawn-out period. And amazingly, that crisis [his "best mistake" story] came right at the end, which is just what happens in the world of stock market patterns—you get the recession or the war at the end of the correction."

Bob Prechter's Best Mistake, in His Own Words

In the early 1990s, the retail investment publishing business was fading, and I decided to counter the trend in declining revenues by having my company, Elliott Wave International, publish analysis for institutions such as banks, insurance companies, and pension funds. As it turned out, institutions became kings in the 1990s, so this decision kept us growing while many retail-only analytical services were going out of business.

To start this new division, I hired outside analysts who specialized in various markets—for example, currencies, interest rates, and international stock markets. We built slowly but persistently toward 24-hour coverage of all major markets around the world. I did the hiring bit by bit, as we grew.

In order to sell these new services, I had to build a sales department, because institutions rarely respond to marketing but prefer phone calls, presentations, and personal visits. To attract the initial people for this start-up venture, I paid the first analysts high salaries and set up some participation agreements. If we succeeded, their pay would go way up. It was how I would have wanted to be paid if I were on the other side of the desk.

As the retail side languished, our institutional side grew. By 1999, we had about a dozen analysts covering institutional services and as many full-time sales personnel. But sometimes persistent growth breeds feelings of entitlement.

Dissatisfaction in the institutional division began in the second quarter of 1999. My CEO had resigned earlier that year, and I began to take stock, finding practices I didn't like and reining in bloat. For example, the sales department was taking overseas sales trips that chalked up expenses for fun times yet brought home few usable leads. I found bills for triple cappuccinos, in-room minibars, a bullfight, a golf club, and a limo ride. Still, I believed that their justifications were sincere and did not suspect a malicious mind-set. The head of sales, I later learned, did not appreciate the new oversight.

Around the second quarter of the year, we had a small dip in sales. The analysts with the highest incomes resented the slip of a few percent in their participation pay. Their attitude made no sense to me, as I knew they could not earn equal paychecks elsewhere. I did not imagine that reasonable people would have a negative reaction to such a normal event. But some of them had taken out large mortgages and had otherwise gotten used to having money flow in at an increasing rate. This shift in conditions turned out to have immensely negative implications for these employees' attitudes toward me and the company.

Around this time, the head of sales and a highly placed analyst, despite the existence of restrictive covenants, began plotting with a competitor and some shadowy financial-business people on how to steal my institutional division. They began by cooking up a get-rich scenario with which to woo the rest of our institutional analysts and salespeople. They would form a new company and give each of them shares. To get the analysts on board, they spent the summer subtly frightening them into believing that my company was going under. The slip in revenues and pay for one quarter and then the next apparently made the claim sound plausible. Later, we found a deleted e-mail from the head of sales telling analysts that they might not get paid for the then-current period but that he was fighting for their rights and well-being. We later learned that he privately advised them not to ask me about the company's downhill slide because I would just lie about it. Paranoia gripped many of the institutional analysts, all entirely unbeknownst to me. None of them came to talk to me about it, because they were told that any defectors would be barred from working with the new group. Members of this chosen group, they were told, would get unbelievably rich after the coup, while I would go almost immediately bankrupt. In other words, anyone who ratted or stayed behind would lose his job. The combination of threat and opportunity placed a very effective clamp on people's tongues.

The plotters put together a plan to steal our customer list and take all our key institutional-division employees simultaneously. They rented hotel space to hold a secret meeting. The external confederates flew in and made a PowerPoint presentation detailing how rich they would all become. It all rested, they said, on keeping quiet until the time came for the key analysts and salespeople to leave all at once, making my company's Internet analysis suddenly go dark, thereby forcing me to send refunds to all of our institutional customers. This way, I would go broke and be unable to fund a fight. I would also have to lay off almost everyone else in the company. Then the salespeople, set up in the new office, would rush to call all of our old customers, telling them to begin sending their checks to the new group, where all of our institutional analysts now resided. The competitor would supply the seed money. The group already had a lease on an office in a nearby community and had started equipping it with phones and computers. On paper, it seemed like a pretty good plan.

But it had a couple of flaws. The first flaw was that the leaders were arrogant and insisted on leaving behind the people they didn't like or that they had dismissed as incompetent. As I later reeled from the first three unexpected resignations, one of the two excluded salespeople caught wind of the plot and started asking questions. (He is now a company director.) The second flaw was a decision that seemed fiendishly clever: Twenty employees would tender resignations one by one during the last three days of the final week in October, giving an end date of Friday, which meant giving essentially no notice so as to cripple the company in one swoop. They would give phony stories of where they were going, and why, to make it appear, at least at first, as if the decisions had been made individually. They made up these stories and carefully chose the date to ensure that everyone leaving that Friday would get paid full salaries and bonuses for the month, not only to give all of them maximum income but also to weaken the company financially. But this timetable ended up turning what would have been a total surprise into only a near-total surprise, and that difference was crucial.

I learned about the plot shortly after the third notice—on Wednesday—of a Friday termination. So, their desire to dissemble their intent by staggering the resignations, but more important to get paid on Friday, gave me one business day to figure out what to do and how to do it.

By pure luck, a highly competent lawyer friend who often travels was in town and available. We spoke on Thursday as more resignations came in. On his advice, on Friday morning I quietly set him up, along with one of his colleagues and three loyal directors from other departments, in a corner office by a stairwell. As the resignations came in, I told each resigning employee that he could collect his paycheck from the accounting department after participating in an exit interview, which was standard procedure. But in this case the interview was designed to learn what was going on. After the first person was interviewed, he was escorted down the stairwell and told not to return. To make sure those already gone could not call in warnings (this was before the era of cell phones), we shut down the office telephones and announced a breakdown of the system. The information technology (IT) department bustled around as if trying to fix it. Upon each new resignation, I chatted calmly with the employee, awaiting the signal that the interview room was available. Some of the conversations had to go on for an hour. It was a grueling day, but one by one, over the course of a 12-hour day from 9 A.M. to 9 P.M., the departing people were processed until we had all the information we needed. Knowledge of the stolen customer list gave us enough to take before a judge the following Monday and ask for a 30-day injunction on the group's actions, which he granted.

Still, the institutional division was decimated. We had only one salesperson left, as the one who had discovered the plot was now deployed elsewhere. Fortunately, someone who worked in another department expressed a strong desire to move to sales, so then we had two. (This person turned out to be our top salesperson within a year.) We transferred all the accounts to the two of them. They had to work long hours to service the larger number of customers per person, but they were fine with it because it meant a good paycheck.

We had only a few institutional analysts left, and few of them were equipped to do the level of coverage required. But we raised their pay, moved them to double shifts, and had the retail analysts chip in with overtime as well. A market-seasoned employee from another department wanted to be an analyst and volunteered for one of the vacant positions. We cut portions of institutional services we thought readers could do without and sent out a call to hire new analysts. We hired two within days. We got some complaints from customers during November, as our market coverage was noticeably thinner. We issued a few refunds and subscription extensions, but our coverage was enough to squeak by during the month of severest stress. When December arrived, markets calmed and some customers took vacation time, giving us a slight breather. From there, we built the department back up, one analyst at a time. Eventually, we even hired back a few of the analysts who had left once we determined that they were more victims than perpetrators of the hijacking scheme.

The rest of our employees realized that the plot, had it been successful, would have immediately forced them out on the street, and they were furious about it. They were also focused and determined.

As it turned out, the head organizers who had so deftly persuaded everyone to join their plan had failed to set up the new office properly. Despite having two months to equip it, the phones weren't working and the computers weren't online. Nor did the promised money materialize. When the judge ordered the group to return our customer list, the outside business people slipped back into the woodwork and stranded their compatriots. Later it became clear that the promise of riches had been vastly overstated even if the plan had worked flawlessly. In the end, we went to mediation, and most of the main people involved agreed to pay enough to cover our legal fees in order to avoid going to court. The episode still cost us a lot of money and brought our company to the brink of disaster. But the in-house perpetrators' and their followers' lives were a mess, too. They went from making high salaries to zero. It was an exhausting time.

I blame myself for a good deal of what happened. Obviously I was not in close enough touch with the employees in these two departments. As a market analyst myself, I had friends among our analysts and was always loyal to them, so I was unprepared for their susceptibility to paranoia and willingness to conspire in secret. However, I had never warmed up to most of the salespeople. We talked and had a few laughs, but we weren't buddies. Had I been closer to them or more aware, perhaps I could have averted the disaster. This was my biggest mistake in 30 years of managing my company.

But you know what? It turned out to be a great mistake. A few months later, my lawyer made an observation: "A bunch of overpriced analysts quit, and now you can replace them at market rates." He was right; it was a major silver lining. But that proved to be only half the boon. As it turned out, 1999 was the top year for institutional business. From 2000 to 2003, as the markets fell and the economy went into recession, the entire institutional-analytics industry experienced a flood of service cancellations. It got so bad that our two biggest competitors, whose only business model was selling analysis to institutions, closed their doors. Meanwhile, our retail division was growing again thanks to the market downturn, and we maintained sufficient income to weather the institutional contraction. Within a short period of time, it became clear that we needed only a few salespeople after all. Our new analysts, all good people, were happy to be here and had no presumptions of entitlement. In most cases, they did better work than the people they replaced. And the lower overhead allowed us to keep the high-level coverage going out.

Then I realized an amazing thing: Given the worldwide collapse in institutional business in 2000–2003, the high cost of our analytical and sales departments under the old model would have driven the whole division into the red. The attempted coup had in fact cleared the decks for us. As a result, I avoided the pain of having to deal with the problems and resentment that would have attended the contraction of the division and the necessary spending cuts that would have gone with it. Soon afterward, I decided that our future was in marketing, not sales, and proceeded to bring in good people to expand our marketing team. A few years later, I dissolved the sales department entirely, finding other slots in the company for the people who had kept it going. As horrible as the three months following the attempted coup had been, the swift contraction in these departments probably saved the company from having three difficult *years*. In retrospect, the timing of the coup was a subtle sell signal for institutional business, as the organizers had operated on the foregone conclusion that the old uptrend would continue apace, which is exactly how people think when a financial market is topping out.

When the dust had settled on this incident, I started a program of e-mailing in-house company news—covering good news and bad as soon as we had it—to every employee. I didn't want them to hear anything at the water cooler that they had not already heard from me. And when they did hear something that didn't sound right, they would know it. We still offer high-level market coverage, but we no longer play the game of traveling, presenting, entertaining, generating sales commissions, and all the other stuff that goes with it. On the Web we built a simple menu for subscriptions under which anyone who wants to can subscribe to what we call our Specialty Services. We sell them through low-key, opt-in marketing. This also helps us keep prices down.

The old sales model flat-out died. But instead of my having to kill it, it committed suicide. All in all, in the end, it was not a disaster but a relief.

Today we have more good analysts, better marketing, and consistent growth. I will always be thankful that I started the institutional division, because it kept my company prosperous during a decade of sharply shifted focus in the financial services marketplace. But I am even more thankful that it blew up. It's a good thing I was too dumb to see it coming.

About Robert Prechter

Robert Prechter has written 13 books on finance, beginning with *Elliott Wave Principle* in 1978, which predicted a 1920s-style stock market boom. His 2002 book, *Conquer the Crash*, predicted the current crisis. Prechter's latest interest is a new approach to social science, which he outlined in *Socionomics—The Science of History and Social Prediction*, published in 2003. In July 2007, the *Journal of Behavioral Finance* published "The Financial/Economic Dichotomy: A Socionomic Perspective," a paper by Prechter and his colleague, Dr. Wayne Parker. Prechter has made presentations on his socionomic theory to the London School of Economics, Georgia Tech, MIT, the State University of New York (SUNY), and academic conferences.

Part Two
Chief Executives

There are people within every organization who actually run the show. For the purpose of the book, I've called them "chief executives."

I originally thought about calling the section "CEOs," but the position of CEO is an implied corporate position, while privately held business entities may call them something else (general manager, president, managing partner, etc.). Besides, one thing I've learned working in the corporate world is that titles don't always tell you what somebody does. There are CEOs who are removed from the company on a daily basis but make the big calls, and others who have their fingers on the pulse of what makes the company run.

There are pat-on-the-back keep-up-the-good-work titles, and there are titles that keep executives at a company but strip them of any power to actually make decisions. You usually find them in that office a little out of the way, with pictures on the wall of themselves with famous people from back in the glory days, and they come in a little less often than they used to and they aren't in those big meetings anymore. And the stories they tell start to sound familiar.

And there are CEOs who make tens of millions of dollars a year but claim to have no idea what's going on underneath them as the company sets up offshore accounts to hide losses in order to make the company look more profitable, and cash in their options as they tell their employees everything's all right and to stay the course in their 401(k)s even as the stock continues to plummet—you know, like Kenneth Lay, who, legally speaking, never did a thing wrong. But I digress.

And then there are *Los Grandes Jefes*.

The people here have actually run companies regardless of their titles. And one of the characteristics of these folks is that they're usually pretty good at managing people. They manage teams toward a common goal and achieve something significant. They've assessed the market, made hard decisions, and reaped the rewards for the company and themselves when things went right. And they've suffered the consequences when things went wrong.

Working chief executives who are not looking back at storied careers—yet—may not be as inclined to talk about mistakes as those who are looking back at long careers. But their experiences of still working and making decisions on a daily basis make their thoughts valuable and extremely relevant in the here and now. I've appreciated the participation of all of the folks here.

Chapter 9
ARTHUR BLANK

Co-founder of The Home Depot

Owner of the Atlanta Falcons

Founder of the AMB Family Foundation

Arthur Blank may have learned many lessons in his business career, but he taught a huge one that should be learned by every executive who makes personnel decisions:

If you're going to fire someone, make sure they can't come back and put you out of business.

Blank and his colleague Bernie Marcus essentially did just that to Handy Dan Home Improvement Centers, a California hardware chain specializing in providing the tools and materials to fix up or repair things around your house. A political battle evolved in upper management, with Blank and Marcus on the losing end. They were fired.

Almost immediately they put their heads together and dreamed up an idea for a home improvement hardware chain called The Home Depot. The idea was to do everything the other hardware store did—but do it better. And there would be one driving value for every employee—excuse me—*associate*.

"You could open up another store that looked exactly like that," Blank says. "Okay, this store is 100,000 feet, this is the merchandise they carry, this is the pricing, this is who they buy from, and so on. But what was unique in our company was the level of customer service inside the store, and the commitment our associates had to taking care of customers."

After 23 years devoting his life to starting up and running one of the most successful retail companies in American history, Blank feels that attention to the customer was the key to its success.

"I always remember a conversation I had with Bob Tillman, who was my counterpart at Lowe's when I was the CEO of Home Depot," Blank recounts. "After Bob retired, and he told me once, 'You know, we modeled our stores after yours, but what we could never understand was how you could get all your store associates to believe in this unique culture of yours that said *the customer's first.*'"

Blank himself may have had something to do with that. He is a Queens-born New Yorker who lost his father at the age of 15. Both he and Marcus came from lower-middle-class families with grandparents who immigrated to the United States from Europe. He was raised in a one-bedroom apartment and lived with his brother until he graduated from college. The sense of never taking anything for granted was transferred to his business.

"We had the sense of constantly having to run," he says, "of always looking for what can go wrong—that sense of always looking out for an issue out there that we're not paying attention to, that there's something around the corner that can get us. And our ability and willingness to see around the corner—for issues or opportunities—was very important toward the success of the company.

"We'd have store meetings or meetings at our store support center," he continues, "and if you had attended these meetings you'd have thought this company was in trouble. We always ran scared; we were always looking over our shoulder. We were always concerned about the competition. We were concerned about responding to the customer. So even though we had this company growing 45 percent a year, earning 48 percent a year, the stock growing 47 or 48 percent a year for 23 years, you would never think that, based on our attitude, or actions, or our language."

In fact, every employee in corporate America could learn something from the process Blank used for choosing those who got promotions and had great careers at the retail giant. And it all had to do with the value of "customer first"—but not because of the value in and of itself, but because of its place in Home Depot's corporate culture:

> We only promoted people in our company—store managers, regional managers, district managers, regional vice presidents, whatever it may be—who believed in that culture. So their ability to do their task well was secondary to their ability first and foremost to live the culture of the company.

When he was CEO at The Home Depot, Blank was one of the biggest employers in the country. Now as the proud owner of the Atlanta Falcons, he has some of the biggest *employees* in the country. Quite a few of them weigh over 300 pounds. I asked him whether he watches a football game and thinks about making changes when somebody does something that drives him nuts.

"Naw," he says. "I've got good people making those kinds of decisions."

It must not be easy for a businessman with so much success to keep his hands off an enterprise that is as public as a football team. After all, it was his sturdy and relentless guidance that helped play a role in The Home Depot becoming a household name.

And it was his willingness to learn from a mistake early on that helped contribute to Home Depot's growth in market share and profits.

The best mistake came in 1984, as the company decided to expand into the Dallas market and take over a company named Bowater, which had nine stores in the area. The move taught them lessons that helped The Home Depot become the classic American success story that it is.

The lessons learned helped the hardware store become legendary for its expansion in stores and profit.

Arthur Blank's Best Mistake, in His Own Words

We spent the first couple of years, between 1979 and 1981, refining the model. We had only four stores in operation. So by 1984, we were still a fairly small company. We had 23 stores then. So the next market we were looking at was Dallas with this company called Bowater. It had made a play early on to invest in our company. It had opened up stores that were somewhat similar to ours in terms of size and what have you in Dallas and several other markets. They had nine stores they were operating.

So when we went to visit the stores we realized they weren't being very well run. They didn't have good service, and they had a lot of old inventory, and the stores looked shelf-worn and shopworn.

We were pretty confident in our abilities. And we thought this would be a way to greatly accelerate our growth. If we could get the company at the right price, we could convert the stores, et cetera. So we did the acquisition.

 One of the mistakes we made in trying to fix these nine (former Bowater) stores is that we took some of the best people we had out of the 23 stores we were running at the time. So we really weakened our existing business in terms of its own ability to continue to go forward and sustain itself.

And even though the stores were doing about half the volume of ours, we thought we could remerchandise and fix the stores while they were open and operating. And the analogy I would make is that it is like trying to change tires on a car going 60 miles an hour. It was very painful.

The stores were in disarray. You didn't have a great customer experience during that period of time. Suppliers were really taxed trying to support us while we were changing the stores. So that was really not a very wise decision.

The third thing we did wrong was we didn't understand how important the culture was in our company. We thought we could change their culture more easily than we actually could. That was in terms of our philosophy of running the business, our customer service philosophy—where the customer was more important than the store and the associates.

 We couldn't get their store managers out of the office onto the floor of the stores taking care of customers. We had one of our district managers go into one of their stores and actually take a forklift and just knock down a store manager's office!

The point was that we wanted store managers out there helping customers and not sitting behind a desk looking at reams of reports.

The fourth thing that happened was that we lost a certain amount of credibility and trust we had established on Wall Street. On Wall Street, credibility and trust are critical in terms of supporting P/E ratios and understanding and believing what management is telling them. We thought we could convert these stores more easily, and it took us several years longer to do it—longer than what we had committed to Wall Street.

So at the end of the day we got it all done. We got the stores remerchandised, and increased the volumes by well over a hundred percent.

We took responsibility for the mistakes. We didn't blame it on the economy or anything like that. We just said we didn't do this well.

Most importantly, we learned some key lessons from it. Even though we were confident as a group of individuals, we developed a sense of humility in ourselves and the company. And we really understood that if we were ever involved in that situation again what we would do differently.

Here were the lessons . . .

Number one, we understood the need to have more balanced growth in the future. Because we are fairly aggressive, Bernie and myself, we actually asked our board of directors to impose a rule on us. Because of the way we were adding stores, we agreed that we would not grow the company more than 25 percent per year. And we had to balance that out in terms of geography, and in terms of the number of new stores in new markets versus old markets, et cetera. That protected us and the company, and the board was happy to oblige.

The second thing is that we took much more seriously the complexity and the challenge of converting the culture of the existing company we were buying to one that was so unique in our company, because in retailing, our orientation was very different than almost anyplace else in America. So we became much more cautious in that regard.

Third, we had to control our expansion. If that meant we couldn't get into our next market more quickly, then we just had to wait. For instance, we had to delay going into Detroit for a number of years. That was not in our personality or the personality of the company. But we did it because we had to make sure we had the kind of focus that we needed.

The Bowater thing was a reinforcement of humility for us—kind of like our head coach saying to our players after an 11–5 record and a run in the playoffs, success can bring both a sense of arrogance and an ego that is inflated. So we became very cautious as a result of that.

All the wonderful press clippings we got for the 23 years when I was there and Bernie was there, we never read them really seriously. We read them, but we didn't post them. We didn't have them as wallpaper on our offices, because we knew we had to focus on the issues I've mentioned.

 It was far cheaper for us to go in and compete with somebody and eliminate them from the marketplace . . . than to go in and buy the business and then convert it.

About Arthur Blank

Arthur M. Blank is the owner and CEO of the Atlanta Falcons. Since acquiring the franchise in February 2002, he has made significant changes that have created renewed excitement for Falcons fans across the region.

During Blank's first year as owner, the Falcons generated a 100 percent increase in season ticket sales (the highest single-year increase in season ticket sales in National Football League history), began a streak of 56 consecutive sold-out games, and built the franchise's first season ticket waiting list. Blank has distinguished himself as one of the most innovative and progressive owners in all of professional sports, allowing him to attract and retain some of the most talented executives, coaches, and players in the NFL.

Blank is also chairman, president, and CEO of AMB Group, LLC, and chairman of the Arthur M. Blank Family Foundation. Both companies are part of the Arthur M. Blank Family Office, with the common purpose of giving back to society through financial contributions and personal involvement.

Blank is widely known in the business community for his success in building the world's largest home improvement retailer. He co-founded The Home Depot in 1978 and retired from the company as co-chairman in 2001. At the time of his retirement, The Home Depot was a component of the Dow Jones Industrial Average and one of *Fortune* magazine's "Global Most Admired Companies." During Blank's last year as CEO of the company, The Home Depot ranked first in social responsibility in an annual survey conducted by Harris Interactive, Inc.

Blank believes in the importance of making a difference—professionally and personally. In addition to the company's financial success, during his 23 years with The Home Depot the company donated more than $113 million to communities, and Home Depot associates provided hundreds of thousands of hours of personal volunteer time. Blank is applying the same business acumen and values to the Atlanta Falcons in building a competitive, successful, and community-oriented franchise.

Blank is also dedicated to his own giving back. Through his generosity, the Arthur M. Blank Family Foundation, along with Blank and his wife's personal giving, has granted more than $250 million to various nonprofit organizations, most recently in Atlanta; Maricopa County, Arizona; Beaufort County, South Carolina; and Park and Gallatin Counties in Montana. Mr. and Mrs. Blank were named as the 2000 Georgia Philanthropists of the Year by the National Society of Fundraising Executives.

Blank is recognized throughout the country for his personal and professional achievements. In 2008, he received an honorary doctor of humane letters degree from the University of South Carolina–Beaufort, and in 2006 he was named Distinguished American by the Walter Camp Football Foundation, which every year recognizes an individual who has utilized his or her talents to attain great success in business, private life, or public service. Also in 2006, Blank was inducted into the Junior Achievement U.S. Business Hall of Fame, and was awarded an honorary degree of doctor of humanities from Furman University. In 2005 he was named National Entrepreneur of the Year by Ernst & Young.

In 2003, for the second time in three years, Blank was named Georgia's Most Respected CEO by *Georgia Trend* magazine, and in 2002 he was inducted into Georgia State University's Business Hall of Fame. Among other previous honors, Babson College inducted Blank into its Academy of Distinguished Entrepreneurs in 1995 and conferred on him an honorary degree of doctor of laws in 1998.

Blank serves on a number of boards, including Outward Bound USA; the board of trustees of the Carter Center, Inc.; the board of trustees of Emory University; the board of trustees of the Cooper Institute; and the boards of Cox Enterprises, Inc. and Staples, Inc.

In September 2001, Blank joined the faculty of Emory University's Goizueta Business School as its first Distinguished Executive in Residence. He now serves as a Goizueta Executive Fellow. Blank also served as the 2003 chairman of the Metro Atlanta Chamber of Commerce.

A native of Flushing, New York, Blank received a BS degree in business administration with distinction from Babson College, where he was active in a wide variety of extracurricular activities.

Blank has six children and two grandchildren. He and his wife, Stephanie, and three of their children live in Atlanta. A strong believer in work-life balance, Blank still makes time for working out. His favorite T-shirt appropriately reads, "There is no finish line."

Chapter 10
DAVID NOVAK

CEO of Yum! Brands, Inc.

Author of *The Education of an Accidental CEO*

Former top-level executive at PepsiCo

A lot of successful people are smart, driven, and have a sense of urgency. While those are all great traits, I think what separates them, and helps people be all they can be, is to be an avid learner," says David Novak. And the Chairman and CEO of Yum! Brands has done a lot of learning over the years. Most of it, though, has been in hands-on roles, making critical decisions while talking to people face to face in the marketplace (after all, Yum! is a fast-food—excuse me, *quick-service*—restaurant company). It didn't come in the halls of Ivy League institutions where the pedigrees of business knowledge are traditionally bestowed. He proudly touts his modest roots, growing up in 32 trailer parks and living in 23 states by the time he was in the seventh grade. He says:

I actually think I got a Harvard MBA. I got the training, without the education. I had raw talent, but I was blessed enough to work with people who could pass on their learning, and I was a sponge for it.

Now he runs the world's largest restaurant company with more than 37,000 units and 1.4 million team members in over 110 countries. The household names include Taco Bell, KFC, Pizza Hut, Long John Silver's, and A&W All-American Food. Yum! revenues were nearly $11 billion in 2009. This is a big company.

"I was fortunate enough to be in a field and get into a career where I actually loved what I do," Novak says. "So it was no problem learning about it. I wanted to learn about it. It was like a hobby to me. And then when you have people mold you, coach you, and help you—that's a big break in life. And that's something that I really couldn't plan."

In fact, his success—and the success of the company he leads—may come down to his ability to read people. "What my background provided me was much better instincts about people. I may be able to get to the core and size up situations maybe a little quicker than other people."

And he believes in motivating them, too. Using reward and recognition to drive results is key to Novak's management style, and he has built Yum!'s entire global culture around it. He created fun awards such as a floppy rubber chicken when he was president of KFC, a cheese head when he was president of Pizza Hut, and his current Yum! Award, an oversized set of walking teeth for employees who "Walk the Talk" of leadership. Fulfilling the human need of workers to feel connected is one of the key tenets in his motivational speeches. From his book, *The Education of an Accidental CEO*:

> It doesn't matter whether you're dealing with a highly ranked executive or someone who's taking orders in a restaurant, you can never underestimate the power of telling someone they're doing a good job.

But how do you motivate employees within a company so big that you can't physically be in a location on a frequent basis? You hire the right people and make them accountable. Novak says:

> Every one of our businesses has a president or a general manager, and functional leaders, and people below them that support our restaurants. When people are doing their job, you let them run the business, and you flex your leadership style depending on whether somebody needs the help or not.

Novak sums it up: "I think when you have a multinational company the most important thing you have to recognize is that building 'people capability' has to be your number one priority. I always say, show me a good business, and I'll show you a good leader."

David Novak's Best Mistake, in His Own Words

I think the best idea I ever had that didn't work was when I was running marketing and sales for Pepsi. I had just come in from Pizza Hut. In the previous four years we had doubled sales and profits. We had a great advertising campaign, great marketing, and lots of new products at Pizza Hut, so Roger Enrico plucked me out of Pizza Hut and said, "You're going to go run marketing and sales at Pepsi," which was a big job.

So I went into the situation, and looked back at all the things that had worked in the category, and it was *new products*—like the introduction of "Diet" products, or packaging innovations like two-liter bottles or 24 packs, things like that. But at the time, PepsiCo was really focused on trying to find the next Michael Jackson, the next celebrity to advertise the product. They had used Madonna and M. C. Hammer versus trying to get at the substance.

But when I went back to see what had really driven the business, it was really new packaging and new products. So I wanted to put my focus on those two things.

On the product front, what I saw was that Pepsi sales were down. And one of the reasons was that there were these emerging alternative beverages, like Clearly Canadian, and bottled water, and all other kinds of alternative beverages, and people were substituting these other kinds of drinks for Pepsi.

 I noticed that the most popular products were all clear. And I was sitting in my office one day and I thought, why don't we just do a clear Pepsi? I got really excited about this idea. I thought what a breakthrough in the category a clear Pepsi with no caffeine would be, and we'll introduce a product like that!

Well, we went out did some research on it, and consumers loved the idea. We had a product that was good; they liked the taste of the product; it was very novel; everybody said they would try it. Of course Pepsi is one of the legendary brand names of the world, so when Pepsi comes out with something dramatic like that, you know at least everybody's going to try it.

We developed this product further. It was a lighter cola taste, with Pepsi notes. We called it Crystal Pepsi. We went in to test-market in Colorado, and it was an overwhelming success. It was a lead story on CBS News, that we were creating a clear Pepsi. People were shipping cases of Crystal Pepsi just like they used to ship Coors beer to where you couldn't get it, because it was a real novelty and people wanted to try it. The thing was huge.

I'd also done the focus groups and it was great, and the initial test-market results were great, but I hadn't really done this with input from the franchise bottlers. So I went to the franchise bottlers, gave them a presentation and told them about the results, and they had obviously heard about it, and they said, "There's only one problem, David. We love the idea—it's a great idea—but it doesn't taste enough like Pepsi."

And I said, "Well, it's not supposed to taste exactly like Pepsi, because we want to have a lighter taste. If it tastes exactly like Pepsi, we won't get the incremental volume. This is meant to be a line extension to our portfolio, so it has to be different from Pepsi."

 The franchise bottlers go, "But it doesn't taste enough like Pepsi and you're calling it Pepsi. If you call it Pepsi it's got to taste more like Pepsi." I kept giving them my answer about wanting to add incremental volume—but I really wasn't listening to this.

The other thing was that I really wanted to launch at the Super Bowl. Pepsi always does a big Super Bowl drill, so this is like the fourth quarter and I come in and I really want to make this product go.

 I don't really *want* to listen. I'm in the "go" mode. I already have enough conviction around this thing that we were going to go national with it.

We move forward. We rush it in to have a national launch. We really wanted to get our business turned around, because it was not doing well. This was my answer to turning around the business.

So we get things geared to launch at the Super Bowl. Now, this is the first product that was ever introduced at a premium price. Usually, Pepsi and Coke have really low pricing. But this was introduced at a premium price by our franchise bottlers.

I asked them, "Why are you doing this?" and they said, "Because it's not going to be around that long."

They thought it was going to be a gimmicky product.

We went ahead and launched the product. But we had a problem with the bottling system where the quality control wasn't as good as it needed to be. So it didn't taste as good as the product we had in our labs and what we had in our test markets. It tasted even less like Pepsi when we rolled it out.

People didn't like the product. We got a tremendous trial, but it wasn't well received. And the number one reason was that "it didn't taste enough like Pepsi."

Here's the big thing I learned. A lot of times when you deal with people and you have a big idea, you've got to have conviction because when you have breakthrough ideas, not everybody is going to see it as a breakthrough. So you have to have courage and conviction. I've always said that some people will say it can't be done every step of the way. But you've got to hold true to your convictions to get things done.

 But I learned that while you have to recognize that some people will say it can't be done every step of the way—and you can't let them stop you—you've got to recognize that sometimes they might be right.

I think it takes humility to recognize that they might be right. You have to genuinely listen, understand what those barriers are, what the real issues are, and then you've got to do the homework to make sure that you're right. And I've tried to do that in my career ever since.

In the case of Crystal Pepsi, it was the best idea that had been developed in the beverage category for years. And what you're seeing right now is all these flavor extensions in the marketplace right now, so the idea was way ahead of its time. But I didn't execute it well because I didn't listen.

Q.   Since there's always somebody who's going to fight you every step of the way, was it the *amount* of negative feedback you got that should have been a red flag?

I think it was that the franchisees were pretty united in the fact that we could create a better product. And I was too focused on making it happen. My sense of urgency, my desire to turn the business around, my passion, conviction—all those things that a really good leader needs to have—all worked against me in that case. As someone once said, your best traits can also be your worst traits. Nothing slowed me down enough to truly listen.

I could have been a part of one of the biggest ideas in the beverage category ever introduced if I had taken the time to get the product right. It could have been a home run. I'll never know.

About David Novak

David C. Novak is chairman and CEO of Yum! Brands, Inc. (NYSE: YUM), the world's largest restaurant company in terms of system restaurants, with more than 37,000 restaurants in more than 110 countries and territories. In 2009, Yum! Brands generated nearly $11 billion in total revenues, including company sales and franchise fees.

Four of the company's restaurant brands—KFC, Pizza Hut, Taco Bell, and Long John Silver's—are the global leaders of the chicken, pizza, Mexican-style food, and quick-service seafood categories, respectively. Yum! Brands employs more than 1.4 million company employees and franchise associates across its worldwide system. Outside the United States in 2009, the Yum! Brands system opened more than four new restaurants each day of the year, making it a leader in international retail development.

Novak shapes the company's overall strategic direction, including four key growth strategies: (1) build leading brands across China in every significant category; (2) drive aggressive international expansion and build strong brands everywhere; (3) dramatically improve U.S. brand positions, consistency, and returns; and (4) drive industry-leading, long-term shareholder and franchisee value. Since its spin-off from PepsiCo in 1997, Yum! Brands has established itself as a global powerhouse going from approximately 20 percent of its profits coming outside the United States to more than 60 percent, while driving one of the highest returns on invested capital in the restaurant industry.

In addition, Novak devotes much of his time each year to personally presenting leadership skills training to the company's management and franchisees, emphasizing teamwork and a belief in people that rewards and recognizes customer-focused behavior, with his trademarked *Taking People With You* program.

Prior to leading Yum! Brands, Novak was president at both KFC and Pizza Hut. He also held senior management positions at the Pepsi-Cola Company, including chief operating officer, and executive vice president of marketing and sales.

Reporting to Novak are the presidents of Yum! Brands' international and China divisions and senior corporate officers. Novak is on the board of directors of JPMorgan Chase & Company, the Yum! Brands Foundation, and the Friends of the World Food Program. He is also a member of The Business Council and the American Society for Corporate Executives. Novak devotes considerable personal support to the United Nations World Food Programme and Dare to Care Food Bank hunger relief. He is also the recipient of the national 2008 Woodrow Wilson Award for Corporate Citizenship.

Chapter 11
DR. BILL FRIST

Set up organ transplant center at Vanderbilt University

Professor of business and medicine, Vanderbilt University

U.S. Senate majority leader, 2003 to 2007

People who undergo a heart transplant to extend their lives probably don't think about it, but successful organ transplantation is all about learning from mistakes. Dr. Bill Frist (yes, the former Senate majority leader) helped set up the first organ transplant center at Vanderbilt University.

"Every time you cured one problem," he says, describing the early days of transplantation research, "there was a new problem."

Already a Harvard-educated cardiac surgeon in the early 1980s, Frist spent a year and a half training under Dr. Norman Shumway, a pioneer in the field of heart transplantation, at Stanford University.

"You do a heart transplant and the patient lives for two weeks, and then they have some rejection, but there's no way to diagnose the rejection," Dr. Frist says, touting the scientific approach that Dr. Shumway established at Stanford. "Dr. Shumway would go back to the laboratory and invent an instrument to diagnose rejection—like a biotome, which you would insert into the neck, then into the heart, pull a piece of the heart muscle out, look at it under the microscope, and then you'd get the patient out to six weeks. And then you'd have a problem with infections, so he would go out and invent another combination of immunosuppressant drugs that would make it less likely to get infections."

The enthusiasm in Frist's voice as he talks about heart transplantation reveals a passion that has consumed a major portion of his life and career. His firsthand account of going through the process of accomplishing a successful heart transplant is presented in his book, *Transplant*. It includes getting word of a donor, identifying and choosing which patient on the waiting list will get the heart, traveling in the middle of the night by private jet and waiting helicopter to remove the heart from the donor patient, fighting the traffic from the airport to get back to the hospital with a dying organ, and performing the life-saving surgery itself. It is as riveting as any movie thriller on the big screen.

His passion for treating the heart began in a physiology class in his second year at Harvard Medical School. He describes it as falling under a spell. As he says in *Transplant*, the heart serves a function in the body, just like other organs. "But most of us *feel* the heart working in ways that we believe are beyond physiology. Our hearts race, or skip a beat, or break, we say, and we are gripped by fear, heavy with sadness, filled with joy, lost in love. From remote time, mankind has considered the heart the sanctuary of our emotions."

When Frist set up a heart transplant program at Vanderbilt, he didn't stop there. He set up a program to transplant other organs as well. "What was unique about our program was that it was under one roof, it was centralized, multidisciplinary, five different organs to be transplanted.

"We established a multidisciplinary team," he continues, "a team doing heart transplants, kidney transplants, liver transplants, pancreas transplants, and even bone marrow transplants, and we put them in a single center. And that concept was brand-new. Nobody had ever done that, not even out at Stanford."

And the reason he did that was so they could learn from each other, which they still do today. "They interact with each other," Frist says proudly, now a professor of business and medicine at Vanderbilt University Medical School. "We have everybody under one roof. They're able to walk the hallways, talk about new innovations, talk about the research, talk about the clinical application, and do it in a way that you learn from each other instead of taking a silo approach to transplantation.

"My whole approach was this: Rejection is rejection, and infection is infection, and you shouldn't have five different teams trying to figure out these five different processes when the underlying biological processes are the same."

Yes, it turns out the medical field doesn't dwell on mistakes, but learning from them is built into the scientific process from the get-go. In fact, life-saving procedures owe their advancements to such learning, and Frist has seen it work. He says:

> The scientific process is about being active and learning from it. It's taking data—measurements and metrics—and applying it in a way that makes science and discovery efficient and have value, instead of being serendipitous where things just happen.

But all of Frist's accomplishments in the field of transplantation occurred only because he had to make a life-affecting decision that some may have considered a mistake—especially at the time. What came later was determined by that decision.

Dr. Bill Frist's Best Mistake, in His Own Words

Around 1982, after I had left Nashville and gone to Boston because it was considered the mecca for heart surgery and for innovation in the practice of medicine, I was surprised and disappointed when all seven hospitals and all the academic medical centers got together, and in a very unusual move said, "Because heart transplantation is a new field, and because it's a field that has not been proven, and because it's very expensive, we're going to put a moratorium on doing heart transplants in Boston."

I had just spent the last 10 years of my life there in Boston, all with the goal of being on the cutting edge [of heart transplantation], of being in a creative environment that was pioneering, that would capture evolving science, shape the science, and direct it in a way that would have a clinical good.

It was terribly disappointing. My dreams had been shattered by a public policy decision made by a group of individuals collectively in Boston, which really ran in the opposite direction of where research and science and finding cures to fatal problems were going.

The decision was made by group of hospitals and clinicians whom I had always looked up to. And all of a sudden they were saying no to what in my mind was one of the most exciting fields in medicine today.

 To be able to take individuals who would be dead in six months, and give them 10, 20, 30, or 40 years of life—the potential for that was a great dream of mine.

And this moratorium occurred despite the fact it was the place that had a history of that sort of thing [innovation in heart surgery], that should have been most interested in it. But they were saying, "No, we're not going to do it. It costs too much. Let somebody else prove it."

Karyn and I had one child at the time, and we had to make a big decision: whether to go on the track to full professor at Harvard, which is a pretty certain track if you stay on it, with med school, internship, residency, fellowship, assistant professor, and then professor.

 Do we stay with the safety and security of Boston, and professorships and clinical directorships there, or do we follow our dreams and follow our hopes of being able to find cures that heretofore had not been either discovered or applied?

We had to make a decision to leave.

At that time, only one person in the country had been working on heart transplants in a systematic, concerted, focused way, beginning with research and carrying it through to clinical application, and that was a guy by the name of Norman Shumway, and he was at Stanford at the time.

So we picked up and left Boston, and left the opportunity to stay there, to go to Stanford to be a senior fellow in transplant surgery, to learn how to do heart transplants. The first successful human heart transplant was performed by Dr. Christiaan Barnard, but it was really based on all the research by Norman Shumway.

The Shumway approach was relying on science. Shumway was very systematic, he was very focused.

 And that sort of systematic approach to science to cure seemingly insurmountable problems is a lesson that I carried with me that I would never have been exposed to had I stayed in Boston.

You had Shumway out there saying, "Believe it can be done, think about how to do it, and just go do it." In Boston, they basically said, "We're not sure it can be done, and it's too expensive, and we should use these resources elsewhere; therefore, let's not engage in the clinical practice." They were saying the value in heart transplantation doesn't exist, so instead of trying to participate in creating that value, they just said, "No, let's put the money elsewhere."

 The lesson for individuals is that if you run up against a roadblock where people say no, and you really believe in it and have the passion that they should not be saying no, you just need to follow your passion and go do it.

If it means leaving the security of a safe, comfortable 30- or 40-year career—as I did—and taking that chance, and going out with somebody who is an iconoclast in some ways, and not even yet accepted in the mainstream, like Norman Shumway at the time, follow that passion, follow those dreams, and realize what can be done.

About William H. Frist, MD

Doctor and Senator Bill Frist is both a nationally recognized heart and lung transplant surgeon and a former U.S. Senate majority leader. Currently Professor of business and medicine at Vanderbilt University, he is uniquely qualified to discuss the challenges and solutions in health care policy. Senator Frist is consistently recognized among the most influential leaders in American health care and is one of only two individuals to rank in the top 10 of each of the five inaugural *Modern Healthcare* magazine annual surveys of the most powerful people in health care in the United States.

Senator Frist majored in health policy at Princeton University's Woodrow Wilson School of Public and International Affairs before graduating with honors from Harvard Medical School and completing surgical training at Massachusetts General Hospital and Stanford University. As the founder and director of the Vanderbilt Multi-Organ Transplant Center, he has performed more than 150 heart and lung transplants and is the author of over 100 peer-reviewed medical articles and chapters, over 400 newspaper articles, and seven books on topics such as bioterrorism, transplantation, and leadership. He is board certified in both general and heart surgery.

Dr. Frist represented Tennessee in the U.S. Senate for 12 years, where he served on both committees responsible for writing health legislation (Health and Finance). He was elected majority leader of the Senate, having served fewer total years in Congress than any person chosen to lead that body in history.

His leadership was instrumental in passage of prescription drug legislation and funding to fight HIV at home and globally.

Senator Frist's latest book, *A Heart to Serve: The Passion to Bring Health, Home, and Healing,* is an inspirational treatise on channeling one's passions to serve others through medicine, politics, and global health. In it he discusses how his family shaped his values, his arduous path to leadership and service to others through heart transplantation, his jump to serving a larger community through politics, and his commitment to global health and communities around the world. The reader is treated throughout to a behind-the-scenes, insider's look at his life-saving emergency surgery on General David Petraeus; his unique health care experiences, including his working almost a year for the socialized British National Health Service; and the never before fully told story of his rise to majority leader.

Today Senator Frist is focused on domestic health reform, K–12 education reform, the basic science of heart transplantation, global health policy, economic development in low-income countries, children's health around the world, health care disparities, medical mission work in Sudan, the health of the mountain gorilla, and HIV/AIDS.

Frist currently serves on the Robert Wood Johnson Foundation's Commission to Build a Healthier America, which has directly linked better health to education. This along with other education research led him to create the Tennessee State Collaborative on Reforming Education (SCORE) in 2009, which is a statewide K–12 education initiative working to improve the level of education for Tennessee students.

Dr. Frist regularly leads annual medical mission trips to Africa. He is chair of Save the Children's Survive to Five Campaign and Nashville-based Hope Through Healing Hands. His current board service includes the Kaiser Family Foundation, Millennium Challenge Corporation, Africare, the U.S. Holocaust Museum's Committee on Conscience, the Smithsonian Museum of Natural History, the Center for Strategic and International Studies, and the Harvard Medical School Board of Fellows.

Senator Frist was the 2007–2008 Frederick H. Schultz Professor of International Economic Policy at Princeton University's Woodrow Wilson School of Public and International Affairs. He is a partner in the private equity firm of Cressey and Company. Dr. Frist is married and has three sons, and lives in Nashville.

Chapter 12

BARBARA CORCORAN

Borrowed $1,000 and quit job as waitress to start real estate company, which became The Corcoran Group, one of New York City's largest

Sold company for reported $66 million

Star of ABC's *Shark Tank*

There's something about success that allows a person to say anything they want. For instance, here's how Barbara Corcoran begins her bio, where most people tout their greatest achievements in order to convince the reader what a special person they are: "Barbara Corcoran's credentials include straight Ds in high school and college and 20 jobs by the time she turned 23."

Not the typical "a graduate of Harvard Business School," is it?

But the entry is the epitome of Barbara Corcoran's personality. She is charmingly disarming, and that personality—along with some down-to-earth smarts—has taken her a long way.

Who else could get away with a book title like this? *If You Don't Have Big Breasts, Put Ribbons on Your Pigtails.*

It is her salesmanship, plain and simple, that has gotten her where she is. She created one of New York's biggest real estate brokerages—which she sold for a fortune—and shares some of her business acumen as one of the "sharks" on ABC's *Shark Tank*, where aspiring entrepreneurs seek advice and investment money for their business ideas.

"There's not a business in America," she says on ABC's web site for the TV show, "that starts, and continues, and succeeds, and is able to jump over the obstacles of building a business, unless you have a phenomenal salesman at the helm."

Corcoran's rise to fame and fortune is the stuff of books—and she has written several. The Corcoran Group is now one of New York's biggest real estate brokerages. Barbara Corcoran started it by borrowing $1,000 in the 1970s. She helped build the real estate powerhouse that she sold in 2001 for a reported $66 million. At one time her client roster included Madonna, Jerry Seinfeld, Britney Spears, Richard Gere, and Courtney Cox, just to name a handful.

With a disarming chuckle behind her words, she'll recount her journey from dyslexic D student to one of the most successful real estate brokers the Big Apple has ever seen.

Barbara Corcoran's Best Mistake, in Her Own Words

One mistake I made was back in 1981 when I created the *Corcoran Report*, which was based on 11 sales, our total sales for the year. I typed it up myself. I listed all the sales and added them up and divided by 11, and it came out to $255,000 and I typed next to it, "Average Apartment Price." I sent it out to anyone who wrote for the *New York Times* that day. The mistake I made was putting "Average Apartment Price" on my letterhead. They took it at face value and it was the head of the Real Estate section the following Sunday. It put me on the map in terms of making us a source in the industry. After that, people were calling for facts and figures. And it wasn't even intentional!

 The best mistake I ever made was creating Homes on Tape, or HOT. I spent $73,000 on it, all of my profits from my first profitable year after the real estate recession [of the late 1980s and early 1990s]. I blew it all on Homes on Tape and it never worked.

The concept was a great idea. We would take all of our apartments and send a guy in who would take video of the apartments. Then we put the broker's face at the end of each apartment [video], with a phone number. It was simple. Each apartment was about 30 seconds and we had 87 or 88 apartments on that first tape. The customers wouldn't have to leave their bedrooms or living rooms; they could just say, "Can you send us your apartments?" and we could send it right over or they could pick it up.

But it had an Achilles' heel that I didn't see. By putting my salespeople's faces and individual phone lines next to the property, none of my salespeople wanted to promote it, hand it out, or deliver it. They were afraid their customer would like the next salesman better. The thing is, there are some people that are very attractive and young, some who've been in the business awhile, some who aren't so attractive or are older. . . . So I forgot the most important lesson in my business, which is we're all working together, but we're all competitors.

 What I was able to do was throw it up on this newfangled thing called the Internet—just to save face and act like it wasn't a mistake. Within the first week, which was a good four years before anyone in the industry was even thinking about the Internet, we had our first sale. So what was the worst money spent immediately turned into an early arrival at a new frontier—and it was totally by accident!

My competitors didn't even have web sites for four years or so. So by the time they were up on the Web, we had chat rooms; we had virtual tours; we had tried anything and everything that struck my whimsy. By the time they were just waking up to the advent of the Internet, I was a pro at it. And they never caught up. I was just trying to save face—ego's a wonderful thing.

What I learned from the Homes on Tape fiasco is that when there appears to be, in every sense, a total disaster, right beyond that total picture of disaster, if you can push 5 percent more, there's gold on the other side. It would have been natural to just write my losses off, which a lot of people believe in doing.

 But I found a lesson that if you think "How the hell do I make something good out of this?" all you need is to push a tiny bit more, that tiny 5 or 10 percent, to find something good.

So I found in a lot of things where someone would say, "Write it off," I was the lone voice saying, "Wait, what else can we do with this?"

About Barbara Corcoran

Barbara Corcoran's credentials include straight Ds in high school and college and 20 jobs by the time she turned 23. It was her next job, however, that would make her one of the most successful entrepreneurs in the country, when she borrowed $1,000 from her boyfriend and quit her job as a waitress to start a tiny real estate company in New York City. Over the next 25 years, she would parlay that $1,000 loan into a $5 billion real estate business.

Barbara is the author of *If You Don't Have Big Breasts, Put Ribbons on Your Pigtails*, an unlikely business book that has become a national best seller. In it, Barbara credits her struggles in school and her mother's kitchen-table wisdom for her imagination and her quick-wittedness in the business world. The book is a fresh, frank look at how to succeed in life and business and is as heartwarming as it is smart and motivating. Her second book, *Nextville: Amazing Places to Spend the Rest of Your Life*, is fast on its way to becoming another best seller.

Barbara is a "shark" on ABC's *Shark Tank* and the real estate contributor to NBC's *Today* show. She is also a columnist for *More* magazine, and appears on HGTV's *Top Ten* and on LXTV's *Price Fix*.

As a speaker, Barbara brings her frontlines experience and infectious energy to every group she addresses. Her tell-it-like-it-is attitude is motivational, inspirational, and sometimes outrageous.

Chapter 13
STEVE FORBES

President and CEO, Forbes, Inc.

Editor-in-chief, *Forbes* magazine

Candidate for U.S. president, 1996 and 2000

W ay before Steve Forbes ran for president of the United States, he was opinionated. And he has always liked to share those thoughts. He recalls:

> I would do a news sheet for my classmates in grade school. I remember in one issue I tried to grade my teachers the way they graded me. It never saw the light of day. My father censored it. He said, "You've got enough problems."

That's one of the endearing characteristics of Steve Forbes. The mild-mannered head of Forbes, Inc., with his polite bearing, is not histrionic and doesn't blow you away with hyperbole, but he's determined to put in his two cents' worth.

And that's part of his pattern of surprising you. The best example of doing the unexpected may be what plays out just about every Friday, when, as a regular panelist, he tapes the business show *Forbes on Fox* for the Fox News Channel. After he goes on the air to tout the merits of the flat tax, less government regulation, and more capitalism to solve the world's problems, Steve takes everyone to lunch.

Now, I don't know how much Steve is worth. I've seen estimates that it's somewhere on the order of a half billion dollars, maybe more. Let's just say he doesn't stay up all night worrying about how he's going to take care of the heating bill.

That's why it's refreshing to see where he takes everyone to lunch: Wendy's—the fast-food joint.

I have no idea whether he owns Wendy's stock, and it's not like buying a dozen square cheeseburgers is going to add anything to his portfolio. But it does say something about the man. He goes to Wendy's and blends in with everyone else. Most of the people there don't have any idea who he is. He doesn't do it for the cameras and he doesn't do it because he's running for president, because he's not. Maybe he appreciates the irony. Maybe he gets the joke. Or maybe he just likes the food. Whatever it is, he doesn't care what anybody else thinks. He thinks for himself.

And he has often gone against the grain of current political thought, including during his campaigns for president of the United States in 1996 and 2000. He has consistently pushed for a flat income tax to replace the myriad of brackets and deductions that traditionally have dominated the U.S. tax structure. The average voter may have known nothing about where he stood on any other issue, but they knew that.

But the flat tax efforts have gotten virtually nowhere. At least not yet. Somehow, though, you get the feeling that the issue, and Steve Forbes, won't go away without being heard from again.

Steve Forbes's Best Mistake, in His Own Words

With two other fellows in college, I decided to start a business magazine. I was a sophomore and they were freshmen. It was a quarterly magazine called *Business Today*. The first issue went to 50,000 students around the country, and the second issue to 200,000.

It would give them perspectives on business that they weren't getting—remember, this was the 1960s and the time of campus radicalism.

I had some inflammatory editorials. We came out against some student rioters—we actually said the students were wrong and the police were right! It was not wildly popular on campus [at Princeton University]. In fact, it was highly unpopular because it was pro-business, so we were seen as fascists and stooges of oligarchs and all that nonsense. Some students even burned copies of the magazine! It made for a very different college experience.

 My father told me at the time, "It'll absorb all your time and you won't do much in the classroom." And he was right! I didn't spend much time on academics, and in that sense it was a mistake. But instead of going to college, it was like an on-the-job MBA.

I learned very quickly that things don't just happen. You learn about cash flow, dealing with angry vendors, meeting writing deadlines. At that stage you have no idea of the nitty-gritty it takes to publish something.

There were sleepless nights, bills, deadlines, getting people to work—it was mostly volunteer students, and you couldn't fire them!

It was a never-ending stream of challenges. You learn what pressure is like.

 We didn't make any money at it, either. But our successors figured out that the conference business was the way to keep the thing solvent. Even today they do one or two conferences a year bringing students and business leaders together from around the country.

Sometimes I speak, but I'm not involved with publishing it anymore.

About Steve Forbes

Steve Forbes is president and chief executive officer of Forbes, Inc. and editor-in-chief of *Forbes* magazine.

Since he assumed his position in 1990, the company has launched a variety of new publications and businesses. They include *Forbes FYI*, the irreverent lifestyle supplement; *Forbes Global*, the magazine's international publication; and Chinese, Korean, Japanese, Brazilian, Russian, Arabic, and Hebrew editions of the magazine. Forbes also publishes the *Gilder Technology Report*, as well as a number of investment newsletters.

In 1997 Forbes entered the new-media arena with the launch of Forbes .com. The site now attracts over seven million unique visitors a month and has become the leading destination site for business decision makers and investors.

Other company divisions include Forbes Management Conference Group and Forbes Custom Media.

Steve Forbes is also chairman of the company's American Heritage division, publisher of *American Heritage* magazine and two quarterlies, *American Legacy* and *American Heritage of Invention & Technology*.

The company's flagship publication, *Forbes*, is the nation's leading business magazine, with a circulation of over 900,000. *Forbes* and *Forbes Global* together reach a worldwide audience of nearly five million readers.

Mr. Forbes writes editorials for each issue of *Forbes* under the heading of "Fact and Comment." A widely respected economic prognosticator, he is the only writer to have won the highly prestigious Crystal Owl Award four times. The prize was formerly given by U.S. Steel Corporation to the financial journalist whose economic forecasts for the coming year proved most accurate.

In both 1996 and 2000, Mr. Forbes campaigned vigorously for the Republican nomination for the Presidency. Key to his platform were a flat tax, medical savings accounts, a new Social Security system for working Americans, parental choice of schools for their children, term limits, and a strong national defense. He continues to energetically promote this agenda.

From 1996 to 1999 Steve Forbes was honorary chairman of Americans for Hope, Growth and Opportunity, a grassroots, issues-advocacy organization founded to advance pro-growth, pro-freedom, and pro-family issues. From December 1993 until June 1996, he served as chairman of the board of directors of Empower America, a political reform organization founded by Jack Kemp, Bill Bennett, and Jeane Kirkpatrick.

Mr. Forbes is the author of *A New Birth of Freedom* (Regnery, 1999), a book of bold ideas for the new millennium.

In 1985, President Reagan named Steve Forbes chairman of the bipartisan Board for International Broadcasting (BIB). In this position, Mr. Forbes oversaw the operation of Radio Free Europe and Radio Liberty. Broadcasting behind the Iron Curtain, Radio Free Europe and Radio Liberty were praised by Poland's Lech Walesa as being critical to the struggle against communism. Mr. Forbes was reappointed to his post by President George H.W. Bush and served until 1993.

Steve Forbes was born on July 18, 1947, in Morristown, New Jersey. He graduated cum laude in 1966 from Brooks School in North Andover, Massachusetts. He received a BA in history from Princeton University in 1970. At Princeton, he was the founding editor of *Business Today*, which became the country's largest magazine published by students for students, with a circulation of 200,000. The magazine continues to be published today by Princeton undergraduates.

Mr. Forbes serves on the boards of the Ronald Reagan Presidential Foundation, the Heritage Foundation, and the Foundation for the Defense of Democracies. He is on the Board of Overseers of the Memorial Sloan-Kettering Cancer Center and on the Board of Visitors for the School of Public Policy of Pepperdine University. He served on the board of trustees of Princeton University for 10 years.

Mr. Forbes holds honorary degrees from Lycoming College, Jacksonville University, Heidelberg College, Iona College, Kean College, New York Institute of Technology, Lock Haven University, Westminster College, Francisco Marroquin University (Guatemala), Sacred Heart University, Centenary College, Pepperdine University, Lynn University, Lehigh University, New Hampshire College, Siena College, Universidad Espiritu Santo (Ecuador), Lincoln College, New Bulgarian University, Spring Arbor University, Seton Hall University, Raritan Valley Community College, and Caldwell College.

Chapter 14

DANNY WEGMAN

CEO of Wegmans Food Markets, Inc.

Wegmans ranked by *Consumer Reports* as best grocery chain in 2009

Chosen by *Fortune* as Best Company to Work For in 2005

I n a world full of people who talk a good game, Danny Wegman doesn't.
He actually plays one.

Danny runs one of the highest-quality grocery store chains in the country—in the world, really—and you could see him on the street and not know who he was. But his presence is felt in each Wegmans food market.

"I remember when I started out," Danny says about the early days. "I began working in the produce department and meat department—the butcher shop. And I didn't understand the importance of the front end—dealing with the customer—until then. What you learn up there is incredible service. What's that? Well, you learn first of all to work as a team."

As Danny began working for his father in the 1960s, his personal guiding light came from President John F. Kennedy. "As a young man, back when I was in high school, John Kennedy was President, and I asked myself, what am I going to do with my life? He said, 'Ask not what your country can do for you.

Ask what you can do for your country.' That was his theme for how we would act. As a young man I really wanted to do things that made our community better, made life better for others and help others."

Those values may help explain, despite his position, his modest bearing. He may not mention that he was a star basketball player in high school. He might not tell you that he graduated from Harvard with honors. And if you ever saw him on a golf course, keeping his cool when his ball goes somewhere that surprises even him, his quiet demeanor may not clue you in to the fact that he runs a billion-dollar family business that has a storied history in the food industry.

Danny Wegman's actions speak louder than his words. They also speak louder than his clothes, too, which sometimes takes a little doing. I once played a round of golf with Danny. As I waited for him to arrive, the caddies there told me that they always looked forward to seeing what shirt he would be wearing. His shirts are about the only thing loud on this modest man from upstate New York.

Danny was born in Rochester to a family that had already established a reputation in the food industry. His father, Robert, was a trailblazer. He took over the family business as president in 1950 at the age of 31. Robert's father and his uncle had built a firmly established grocery store in Rochester that played underdog to the A&Ps of the world, but Robert pioneered its growth to the point that it changed the supermarket shopping experience. Robert has been credited with developing and implementing the one-stop-shopping concept that Wegmans stores have become known for. He added things like a pharmacy, a video department, a photo lab, and a child care center. In 1994, a front-page story in the *Wall Street Journal* quoted supermarket industry analyst Neil Stern, who said, "We consider them the best chain in the country, maybe in the world." [*Note:* I had the privilege of interviewing Robert Wegman before his passing in 2006. He had an intellectual curiosity that made him more interested in what you had to say than in expressing his own insightful thoughts about business and world events.]

But even before Robert Wegman's passing, Danny had been essentially running day-to-day operations for years. And he helped expand the company beyond its New York borders, which may have been considered a mistake by some, but Danny knew it was the right thing to do and he did it to enormous success.

Part of the company's success can be attributed to the visceral experience of walking into a Wegmans food store. A violin is just a piece of wood with some strings until it is picked up by Itzhak Perlman. And produce is just food until it's put in a Wegmans grocery store.

Most grocery stores carry produce. Wegmans has rows and rows of fresh fruits and vegetables, some of them bought from local growers and delivered directly to the store.

Most grocery stores sell cheese. Wegmans cheese shops offer up to 500 varieties of cheese from around the world. Wegmans even makes its own fresh cow's milk mozzarella daily, right in the store.

"We appeal to people who have a high food interest," Danny says. "They have an appreciation for different types of food, and have the discerning palate. They want ripe cheese rather than not caring what the cheese tastes like."

Wegmans has a pastry shop designed with the help of a top French chef; offers hundreds of ready-to-eat and ready-to-heat foods to make eating well more convenient; sells its own brand of Food You Feel Good About meats, which have been raised free of antibiotics and hormones; has an in-store Market Café; and some of its 75 stores in five states have a wine shop with wine-tasting events to complete your dining education.

That's just the stuff you eat.

"In almost every product we carry," Danny says, "the taste has to be appreciated. But that's also an educational process."

Then there are the little carts that toddlers push behind their parents with little pennants that read "Customer in Training," or the day care center where you can put the kids while you're shopping (parents probably go there for that even when the fridge is full!). There's the pharmacy, the tableware section, and the numerous checkouts that are probably pretty busy because you won't be the only one in a store that is so popular that some of its biggest customers border on the fanatical.

There's an energy that brings the place alive. When you walk into a Wegmans, you know the difference between it and a regular grocery store. You know you're *somewhere*. People didn't just happen to walk into the immense food market; they went there on purpose.

Then there's the customer service. The people who work there are knowledgeable and appear genuinely interested in trying to make sure you can find what is on your shopping list.

And all of these features are not even what the company has gotten the most headlines for.

It's known as a great place to *work*.

"If our employees are happy," Danny explains, "they'll do anything for our customers."

Fortune chose the company as the Best Company to Work For in 2005. In fact, since the list's inception in 1998, Wegmans has made the list each year and the top 10 for seven consecutive years. The ratings are based on two criteria: the policies and culture of the company, and the opinions of the company's employees. The opinions count for two-thirds of the total score, so obviously Wegmans employees are happy. And that may translate to customer service. Danny says:

> When a customer treats you rudely, you don't treat them rudely back like you might do at home or on the street. You change, and you take putting a smile on that customer's face as a challenge. These are all things you learn on the front end of our store. You think everybody knows these things, but they don't.

> The challenge is: how do you conduct yourself as a person? And as I watch the faces on the front end of our stores, I can see that they're turned on by what they're doing.

The company also has made a commitment to give back to the community. Danny became president of the company—his father continued as CEO—in 1976. And in 1987 they created the Hillside Work-Scholarship Connection, a program that has been very successful in reducing the dropout rate among at-risk students in the Rochester city school district. More than 1,000 middle and high school students participate in the program, and each is provided a youth advocate, part-time job, and workplace mentor at Wegmans and other companies that now participate. President George H.W. Bush presented the Hillside Work-Scholarship Connection with the Grand Prize American Business Press Points of Light Award in 1991.

Danny Wegman explains: "We set out to start a program that would help these kids graduate from high school, and the essence of the program was to come to work at Wegmans. In 2007 we had 130 graduates from this program; 110 are in college two years later. I don't know any university that's got that kind of retention number. Stop and think about it. They were predicted to not make it. These kids were predicted to drop out of school. So the change is pretty shocking.

"With a lot of these kids their parents never graduated from high school. They're on welfare; their role models are pimps, prostitutes, and drug dealers. What they need is someone who has been successful to be a cheerleader and a 'hope provider.' We have around 100 of these folks—we call them 'advocates.' Their role is to provide hope and confidence for these kids that things will work out."

Danny says:

My dad never felt that money was what made you happy. Doing something that was meaningful to you is what made you happy in life.

Danny believes that employee satisfaction can be traced directly to management policies. And he thinks it might be an advantage to employees that Wegmans is not a publicly held company. (Founded in 1916, Wegmans has roughly 38,000 employees in its 73 stores, and sales approaching $5 billion a year.)

Take 2008—the year of the financial meltdown. Danny tells what they decided to do.

Danny Wegman's Best Mistake, in His Own Words

Gas prices were going up enormously in May, and so were food prices because food was connected to gas at the time. There was a shortage of corn and it was pushing up the grain markets, and our employees were having a really hard time with it. First of all, they had to drive to our stores on a daily basis, and second of all was their own cost of food.

So we decided to give them 10 percent off their food purchases for a couple of months. We did that by allowing them to buy gift cards for 10 percent off, which they could then spend on food.

 We didn't look at the cost of it. We said, "We've got to help our people." If we were a public company we might have said, "Gee, we can do that as soon as the year is over and we'll spend the money then, but we want to make our budget." But our whole focus was to *not* lay off employees.

We thought if we're not careful here with this bad economy, business is going to drop, so what can we do to keep the business from dropping?

So in November of 2008, as the economy was reeling from a stock market crash and in the heart of the worst recession since the Great Depression, we lowered our prices.

I've never seen such an emotional response from our customers because other food companies just weren't doing that. As I visited stores during that period of time, it's amazing how people would come up, almost in tears.

That was about a $12 million expenditure. A little while after that, in January 2009, we spent about $15 million reducing pharmacy prices.

If we were a publicly held company, I probably would have lost my job. But as a private company we just don't think that way. We think, what's the right thing to do? And we have total confidence that if we do the right things the numbers will work out.

[And work out they did. The fiscal year 2009, according to Danny, was the best sales and profit year in the company's history.]

 Our customers understood what we did, and they said, "I'm going to shop at Wegmans." Eventually others lowered their margins, but we did it before they did so we got that customer connection.

About Danny Wegman

Danny Wegman is CEO of Wegmans Food Markets, Inc., headquartered in Rochester, New York. Danny graduated with honors from Harvard University with a degree in economics. Aside from Wegmans, Danny remains an active member of the Food Marketing Institute (FMI) and currently serves as chair of FMI's Food Safety Task Force. He is a member of the board of trustees at the University of Rochester, and is involved with the United Way and the Hillside Work-Scholarship Connection, a program founded by Wegmans in 1987, to reduce the dropout rate within the Rochester city school system.

Wegmans Food Markets, Inc., a leading supermarket chain in the Northeast, operates 75 stores in New York, New Jersey, Pennsylvania, Maryland, and Virginia, with annual sales of $4.8 billion in 2008. The company has built an international reputation for its overall excellence in quality, customer service, and variety, and has been named for the 12th consecutive year to *Fortune* magazine's list of the 100 Best Companies to Work for in America. Wegmans is perhaps best known for its high-quality fresh and prepared foods, as well as its wide range of ethnic and specialty foods.

Chapter 15
GARY GOLDBERG

Host of *Money Matters*, one of America's longest-running financial radio talk shows

Founder and CEO of Gary Goldberg Financial Services

Co-author of *High-Powered Investing: A Financial Planner's Guide to Making Money in Today's Uncertain Markets*

Gary Goldberg remembers when he started out as a stockbroker. "My training director said to 'make a list of everybody you know of who is going to do business with you.' I remember filling up my yellow sheet with 28 names. And of those 28 names, only one did business with me and that was my father—and he didn't have any money!"

Gary's ability to tell a story has helped his daily radio show, *Money Matters*, become one of the longest-running financial advice programs on radio.

Every time I would call my dad he'd say, "Okay, buy me a hundred shares." And the stocks were terrible. They all kept going down. One time I called him and he said, "Gary, how much do you make when I buy these stocks?" I told him about a hundred dollars. So he said, "How about if I send you a hundred bucks and you quit calling me?"

His poor-kid-made-good life story starts in the Bronx, and has led him to suburban Suffern, New York, where he runs a money management company that specializes in what he calls the "mass affluent." These are people with money to invest, but not enough to get the attention of private wealth managers at places like Goldman Sachs and JPMorgan Chase.

When he meets with prospective clients, there's an air of experience that comes across that instantly puts the visitor at ease. He doesn't have to say he knows what he's doing. Clients just know it.

In those meetings he is more likely to tell a story about being a poor kid from the Bronx than about the riches he's accumulated as a successful entrepreneur.

"I remember my mom used to take me shopping for shoes. And we'd always go to the department store where they'd have this big bin full of hundreds of shoes. And the pairs would be tied together with about a six-inch string. So my mom would put them on my feet and say, 'Okay, walk in them.' And I'd be shuffling back and forth, taking these tiny little steps trying to walk in them, and she'd say, 'Fine, we'll get those.' I really thought I'd hit the big time when I tried on shoes that weren't tied together."

He started the company in the early 1970s with $5,000, a card table, a phone, and a walk-up office in New City, New York. He would call people and ask if they would like a meeting to review their investment portfolios.

Now he drives a Bentley to those meetings, and wears designer shoes and monogrammed shirts. And it's the result of thousands of sales calls and thousands of investment recommendations that have paid off. (In the spirit of full disclosure, I should mention that I count Gary as a good friend, and for a short time he was my employer.) At a point in his life in which he could easily retire, move to his property in Scottsdale, and not work another day in his life, Gary pushes forward each day with a full schedule of client meetings. And he continues to tell stories.

Like the one about his then 80-something mother living in Florida.

"There was this commotion outside my mom's condo. So she goes out on the balcony and sees a bunch of firefighters yelling up to a girl getting ready to jump from the floor above my mom. So she looks up to the balcony right above her and says to this girl, 'Hey, what are you doing? Why are you going to jump?' The girl says, 'My boyfriend broke up with me and I don't want to live anymore.' My mom says, 'This is over a man?' And the girl says, 'Yes.'

"So my mom says, 'A man! It's not worth it. Wait, don't jump. My son is coming down in a couple of weeks to see me and I'll introduce you. He does very well.'

"The girl goes back into her condo and doesn't jump. The fire department gives my mom this commendation and she gets her picture in the local paper." And he adds, anticipating the question: "No, I never went out with her."

Telling stories is what brings people in, and business acumen and experience are what has allowed Gary Goldberg Financial Services to succeed. And that financial knowledge didn't come without lessons. One of them was his best mistake.

Gary Goldberg's Best Mistake, in His Own Words

I was an institutional broker on Wall Street in the late 1960s. I had just gotten my license so I was starting to make my calls.

I made an appointment with a renowned money manager, Richard Ney. He was a young guy back then. He had an office on Madison Avenue. At the time it was my first research idea. It was AMF, the old billiards and bowling ball company. I finally landed an appointment with him. He said "Fine" and he gave me a date. And the night before my presentation, I remember staying up all night in order to study AMF. I was really flexing my muscles. I felt I knew everything about the company I needed to know, and I went to his office.

He was in this office that I will never forget. It was wood paneled, and he had a backgammon set—it was kind of over the top. He was one of those young Wall Street honchos who had made a big name for himself. So I went through my presentation and I thought I was terrific.

Then he said, "I want to ask you a question." And the first question he asked related to some accounting aspect of the company.

 I had no idea what the answer was. I went ahead and attempted to answer his question, but I didn't know what I was talking about.

So instead of saying, "I'll get you the answer. I don't know, but I'll get back to you," I gave him this answer and I remember the look he gave me after my stellar performance. He said, "You don't know what you're talking about. Get out."

Boy, was there a lesson in that. I've never done that again. There's nothing wrong in saying, "I don't know. I'll go and check with my research department," or "I'll check out the research myself."

But trying to try to fudge it and to come up with answers that don't make sense is a terrible way to go through life, and I never experienced anything like that again.

I never talked to him again. He wouldn't take my calls. I had lost all credibility.

About Gary Goldberg

Gary Goldberg is the founder and chief executive officer of Gary Goldberg Financial Services. As founder and leader of the firm, Mr. Goldberg is the main driving force behind its investment strategy and policy. He is a member of both the firm's Executive Committee and the Strategic Investment Committee. Prior to forming Gary Goldberg Financial Services in 1972, Mr. Goldberg had a successful career as an institutional trader on Wall Street. Since then, he has built the firm bearing his name into one of the premier full-service investment management firms in the Hudson Valley region.

In addition to serving as the firm's CEO, Mr. Goldberg also hosts America's longest continually running financial radio talk show, *Money Matters*. As host of *Money Matters*, Mr. Goldberg is able to interview some of today's most influential political and business leaders, giving him an advantage to gain firsthand insight into their thoughts and feelings about current market and socioeconomic conditions.

Mr. Goldberg earned his bachelor's degree from Bard College and attended Brooklyn Law School.

Chapter 16
JERRY LEVIN

CEO of AOL–Time Warner

Head of Home Box Office (HBO)

Created pay-for-TV-content business model

Back in the 1972, major league pitcher Denny McLain lost 22 games for the Washington Senators. Why would a pitcher be put on the mound enough times to lose that many games? Because two years prior to that he had won 24 games with the Detroit Tigers, and the year before *that* he won 31 games as the Tigers became World Series champions (no one has won 30 games in a season since).

In other words, you have to do something really well to get the opportunity to do something that goes really badly.

Enter Jerry Levin.

The average person couldn't tell you who Jerry Levin is, especially the slimmed-down and tan version of him in Santa Monica, California, where he and his wife operate a high-end mental health clinic and spa. But on Wall Street you can recognize him because when he walks into a room he's got an 800-pound gorilla attached to him. And the gorilla's name is AOL–Time

Warner, as in the failed merger. The business media like to refer to Levin as the "CEO who presided over the worst deal of the century."

But wait a minute. How did he get in a position to put together such a historic combination of old and new media if he was so bad?

Because like a 31-game winner, he had his share of victories in the past.

Here's what the *Los Angeles Times* wrote about Levin in 1992:

> In the mid-1970s, he was widely credited with helping to create the cable television business. It was Levin, as head of the Home Box Office division, who persuaded Time executives to invest $6.5 million in a satellite service that made HBO available to cable television systems nationwide.

In plain language, Jerry Levin helped create the cable TV and satellite TV industries. That is no small feat, because in order to do that, he had to change a TV business model into one based on people *paying for content*.

"With HBO," he recalls, "I was right there at the start. I was actually the first on-air person, and gave it its name. It was not successful right away, but the theory was that we were going to give people programming that they paid for, as opposed to it being supported by advertising, and there had been a graveyard of early pay TV experience that failed." But he pushed ahead and created one of the most successful media business models in history.

If you look at the steps that led to his early success, you can almost see why the AOL–Time Warner merger made sense to him.

- TV content had been free to the viewer. Internet content was mostly free.
- People had a strong desire for TV content particular to their individual interests. It was the same with people on the Internet.
- Eventually television viewers paid subscriptions to cable and satellite providers. AOL had a strong subscriber base paying to get access to the Internet.
- Early attempts at pay TV failed. Early attempts at charging for online content had mostly failed.

Is it any wonder he thought there might be a workable business model in there somewhere?

But back to reality, and the gorilla. The AOL–Time Warner merger turned out to be a financial disaster. At $350 billion, it was the biggest merger in history. Announced on January 10, 2000, the timing of the deal could not have been worse. By May 2000 the dot-com bubble began to burst, and so did the stream of revenue produced by AOL's mostly dial-up subscription list. That meant that a huge component of a workable business model was fatally damaged.

Stockholders lost billions in market value. Ted Turner, as the media looked back at the 10 years since the historic deal, told the *New York Times* that as the largest individual shareholder of the combined company at the time, he alone lost an estimated $8 billion. "The Time Warner–AOL merger should pass into history like the Vietnam War and the Iraq and Afghanistan wars," he said. "It's one of the biggest disasters that have occurred to our country."

The company itself lost tens of billions in market capitalization. Jobs were lost, and the effort to create a transformative combination of old and new media businesses was well on its way to running into the ground. Levin announced his retirement in December 2001, and the companies finally separated in December 2009.

Those are some of the ingredients of what business media have widely dubbed the "Worst Deal of the Century." Levin says,

> What the Internet taught us is the oldest business lesson in the world, and that is, innovation is going to come at a time and from a place that is least expected, and there's going to be creative destruction of existing businesses.

But Levin hopes the AOL–Time Warner experience doesn't deter other business leaders from taking the necessary steps to help a fledgling industry evolve.

> You don't want it to teach us not to take risks. You have to try to continue to innovate and transform. If you build your identity on being perfect, you're just going to tread water; you're not going to innovate. The hallmark of our capitalist system is new ideas, innovative advances that lead to the change in existing industries, and they come at unexpected times—and that's the brilliance of it.

So what can we, as members of the capitalist system, learn from the AOL–Time Warner failure?

Culture Problems

"When you mix cultures, you really need to understand psychology," Levin reflects. "These transactions that are so dramatic actually create some kind of psychological issues and trauma in people. As CEOs you're not even aware of it because you're basically operating at a strategic level; you're not operating at a very human level."

> Basically, with mergers like AOL–Time Warner, it's the frontier of change. It's almost paralyzing to people. I think that's what we missed.

The Bubble

"And how do you know when you're in a bubble?" Levin asks. "It's easy to look back now and know what was happening, but back in the middle of the dot-com exuberance, it was easy to justify outlandish stock valuations because the world was changing. Add to that the complication of being a CEO and meeting the Street's expectations." He continues:

> You just get carried away with growth rates. And it's hard to see when that growth rate is going to stall, particularly when you're growing very rapidly.

One could argue that an experienced CEO like Levin should have recognized a clash of corporate cultures, a classic merger obstacle, but he wasn't alone in being caught up in the bubble.

We at CNBC were passing out "Dow 10,000" hats on the floor of the stock exchange eight months before the AOL–Time Warner announcement. Jim Glassman and Kevin Hassett's book *Dow 36,000* was published in 1999, predicting the stock market would reach that exorbitant level in just a few years. (The Dow reached 14,000 before losing half its value during the financial crisis.)

I recall anchoring a morning show at CNBC called *Today's Business* and interviewing one guest after another who spoke of the great new things being done on the Internet. And the mania affected investment decisions. I asked an established (and still respected) money manager off camera one time, "How can you justify having all those dot-coms in your portfolio?" He said, "I've got to, Bob. The valuations are crazy, but if I don't have them in the portfolio, I'll get killed on performance compared to everyone else."

While there were a handful of voices warning of the danger—my CNBC colleague Ron Insana's comparison of the market to Japan's 1980s asset bubble comes to mind—not many people were getting in the way of the story line of the day, which was this: America was investing its future in the stock market and in dot-coms in particular.

Not surprisingly, the merger announcement itself was met with bubble-like fervor. When CNN/fn (remember them?) reported the news on its web site, the article quoted Scott Ehrens, a media analyst with Bear Stearns (remember them?): "Together, they [AOL and Time Warner] represent an unprecedented power-house. If their mantra is content, this alliance is unbeatable. Now they have this great platform they can cross-fertilize with content and redistribute."

And some of today's biggest critics of the merger were caught up in the excitement of it at the time themselves. From the *New York Times*, January 11, 2000, there was this:

> The man who started CNN two decades ago was Ted Turner, Time Warner's 61-year-old vice chairman and its largest shareholder. Yesterday, Mr. Turner explained his support for the merger.
>
> "When I cast my vote for 100 million shares, I did it with as much excite-ment as I felt the first time I made love some 42 years ago," Mr. Turner said. "I voted for it because we will have a stronger company that will create value. It's not so easy to go out and recreate AOL. No one has been able to do it so far."

So it comes as a slightly disarming show of humility when Levin says, "I certainly apologize for not seeing all this." Apologies are not a common practice among CEOs—even former ones. But it may be more than just a therapeutic step for a man whose spa facility now helps others deal with emotional and psychological trauma. It may be a necessary step toward learning the lessons from business innovation—and teaching them to others who follow.

"If you acknowledge that you make mistakes, it should not be a paralyz-ing loss. Because if you're afraid of making mistakes, then you're not going to barrel through to some kind of new concept. In fact, it's the chain of errors—the stops and starts—which leads to innovation." Levin continues:

> Maybe we shouldn't call them mistakes, because there's a value we get from them. It's part of the pathway of trial and error. Trial and error—and just keep moving.

"Maybe, Bob," he says, "the lesson is that if you don't want to take a huge risk because you're afraid you're going to make a huge mistake—that it's going to be your legacy and you're going to be bothered by that—then we're not going to get anywhere. But if you're prepared to take that kind of risk, *that's* how new businesses are going to take place or be transformed. If you're worried about your position, about how you're going to be viewed—either your stock market perception or your legacy—then you're not going to take risk." He concludes:

> The fact is, everybody's still struggling with the same concept: How do you get the consumer to pay for content? It's probably going to come in some form of subscription that delivers value. I'm also a big believer in subscriptions, but it hasn't quite been understood yet.

Best Mistakes

The irony is that Jerry Levin—sans gorilla—spent years giving a Wall Street presentation about the many mistakes he had made that contributed to his success. He was, after all, the CEO of Time Warner. "These so-called mistakes really informed my strategic view of the world, and it's been a pretty consistent theme. Probably the most significant characteristic was that we were always a little early."

His willingness to blaze paths, the same inclination that led to the AOL–Time Warner mess, also led to great successes. He considers those experiences part of the best mistakes of his business career.

Jerry Levin's Best Mistake(s), in His Own Words

Q. What drove your vision in creating HBO?

At HBO, the idea of giving people choice, as opposed to what the network delivers at its time schedule, was really the fundamental concept. It was relatively primitive at the start. It didn't quite work at first because people weren't accustomed to the concept of pay television. Once you got it in the home and started delivering some programming, it was there.

 From the small auspices of HBO I was driven to give the consumer complete choice, complete convenience, and complete control. That was the hallmark.

It was the same thing with satellite. We went up on the satellite and nobody thought that the cable industry was capable of managing that kind of technology. The idea that you would put a network up full-time on a satellite was beyond the pale because the cable industry was viewed as kind of a backward technology—but it worked.

Q.   What steps did you take to get to the business model that worked for the viewer?

We started to experiment in the late 1970s with cartridge television, the idea that you could play, stop, and replay television.

We had a book of the month club, so we started a movie of the month club.

 But this was before the advent of home VCRs, and they were very clunky machines and the thing failed. But it was clear that if you put some kind of VHS kind of machine in the home that people would like it.

This was Netflix 25 years ahead of its time. But we had to close it down.

The next thing I saw was that we were delivering magazines and newspapers, so why not give the consumer a lot of stuff in the home? We put together a journalistic group, spent $25 million in 1982 and 1983, and sent by satellite into one cable system a lot of Teletext material.

 The problem was there were no computers at the time, so it was not interactive. It was a one-way system. And it was considered a failure. But at least we learned that we needed to give the consumer a lot of information that was interactive.

I think the best example was we set up what we called the full-service network in our cable system in Orlando in the early 1990s, and this really was the precursor to video on demand. Except it was very expensive. We bought the first server—the nonuse of tape—in media history.

One of the main highlights in my career was when we brought the Ali–Frazier fight from Manila by satellite into cable systems in Florida. I remember watching it, and it was really exciting.

The other one was in the early 1990s. We put up in one cable system an interactive service that was digital, and we had a lot of press come in from around the world, and I started to play a movie and I stopped it and started it, backward and forward. It was all done without tape; it was all done through the network, and there were all these ooh's and ahhh's.

This was like 1992 and 1993, but the equipment was just early; the equipment wasn't cost-efficient and we closed it down. And it was branded a failure.

But in fact, with video on demand, all the stuff we used, like the Silicon Graphics software, actually became part of the interactive digital video on demand. But it was a so-called failure, and yet I knew the consumer was there. We saw these people, these families in Orlando, and they loved it.

With the Internet, it was the same thing. We started a service with Time called Pathfinder. It was just a little early and we didn't quite know how much to give the consumer. And that's why I was driven.

 I saw the Internet as the ultimate expression of complete on-demand information and entertainment, which was going to change the business plans of every business around. I thought we needed to be on that bandwagon.

Hence the AOL–Time Warner deal.

What I'm trying to articulate is that all these incidents were strategically connected, like moving DVD along or HDTV, and were part of a trajectory—which began with HBO—to give the consumer total control, choice, and convenience. It's still where the media business is today. That's what led to the Internet (we had a service called Pathfinder in the early 1990s) and eventually the digital makeover of TWX and AOL!

About Jerry Levin

Gerald M. Levin, until May 2002, was the chairman and CEO of Time Warner Inc., at that time the world's largest media and entertainment company, with industry-leading businesses in publishing and news, cable networks, filmed entertainment, cable systems, music, and interactive services.

A recognized pioneer in the development and deployment of digital and interactive media, Levin was the prime mover in the merger of Time Inc. and Warner Communications in 1990, the originator of Time Warner's merger with Turner Broadcasting System and CNN in 1996, and an architect of the merger of AOL and Time Warner in 2001. He became the first sole CEO of Time Warner in December of 1992, and was elected chairman of the board on January 21, 1993.

Levin became CEO of Time Warner in December after being named president and Co-CEO in February 1992. He became CEO of Time Warner in December 1992 after being named president and Co-CEO. He previously had been COO and vice chairman of Time Warner, a position he attained when Time Inc. merged with Warner Communications Inc. At Time Inc., Levin was named vice chairman and elected to the Time Inc. board of directors.

Levin joined Time Inc. in 1972 when Home Box Office, the company's pay-cable subsidiary, was in its developmental phase. He served as HBO's vice president of Programming, was named its president and CEO and was promoted to chairman. Levin made the historic 1975 decision to distribute Home Box Office via satellite, which helped create the modern cable industry.

Previously, Levin was an attorney with the New York City firm of Simpson Thacher & Bartlett, and had been affiliated with Development and Resources Corporation, an international investment and management company, where he became general manager and COO. Following that company's acquisition by International Basic Economy Corporation (IBEC), he served for a year as IBEC representative in Tehran, Iran.

Levin graduated Phi Beta Kappa from Haverford College and received a legal degree from the University of Pennsylvania Law School, where he was note editor of the Law Review. He has received honorary degrees from the University of Vermont, Texas College, Middlebury College, the University of Denver, and Haverford College. He is also former chairman of the board of Haverford College. He is also the former chairman of the board of managers of Haverford College and a Trustee Emeritus of Hampshire College.

Levin served as a director of the New York Stock Exchange as well as the New York Federal Reserve Bank. He was also a member of the board and treasurer of the New York Philharmonic, a board member of the Aspen Institute, the National Cable Television Center, and the Museum of Jewish Heritage. He was on the Council on Foreign Relations, the Trilateral Commission, the Economic Club of New York, and the Council of International Advisers to the Chief Executive of Hong Kong.

Chapter 17

R. J. KIRK

On Forbes 400 list of richest Americans

Co-founded New River Pharmaceuticals—sold for $2.6 billion

Senior managing director and CEO of Third Security, LLC

So there I was, having one of those typical days when you talk with a billionaire about parallel universes.

Excuse me? Yes, that's the kind of conversation that can occur when the wildly successful businessman R. J. Kirk starts talking. He's obviously smart. A law degree from the University of Virginia isn't bestowed on the intellectually lethargic. Nor is success in starting up companies and making tremendous profits from running them and then selling them. No, you don't become a self-made billionaire by pure luck. You must have done something right along the way. That makes it a bit curious when you hear him talk about the keys to success: that there aren't any. Or at least—and I want to pick the right words, because R.J. is very precise—you can't determine them.

"I'm at a loss to explain success," he says. "Just as a matter of proof, it's almost never possible to explain why something succeeded." And he thinks that most rich, successful people overestimate their own brilliance. "They usually draw the wrong inferences from their own success—one of which being there's a temptation to believe one is a great deal more intelligent than one truly is."

Such are the unconventional arguments made by a business professional in a position to comment on careers marked by financial achievement. "By sort of algorithmic fact, we are limited to learning from our failures. It's true in science. It's true logically. I would say it's true tautologically. It's not really possible to learn from a success."

For someone like myself, writing a book about learning from mistakes, I found this a breath of agreeably self-serving air. Still, I couldn't help but feel a little off kilter. I mean, what about all the books and lectures on how to succeed? It's practically an entire genre. Are they of no value whatsoever?

"With success you don't get feedback, so you can't really learn from success," he says. "You can't tell which were the critical factors that contributed to a success. And you can't prove them, because you weren't able to go back in time and alter those inputs and try it the other way."

"So," I say, trying to bring the conversation down to my level, "it's like on *Star Trek* when they're presented with nine different possible universes?"

"I think that's exactly the way a physicist would think about it," he says. "If there was a split universe at every decision point and you only went *this* way, it's not really possible to test the *other* universes.

"When you produce a failure, though," he continues, "It is possible to derive some inferences and therefore to learn from failure."

Failure is not something that has visited R. J. Kirk on a regular basis. His investments and commitments as an entrepreneur led him to co-found General Injectables & Vaccines, a southwestern Virginia next-day provider of medical supplies to doctors. The ownership team sold the company for more than $67 million in 1998.

Then he and some colleagues founded Third Security, a Radford, Virginia–based investment management company that specializes in life sciences. The company invested in a start-up that became New River Pharmaceuticals, which was sold a few years later for a profit that reportedly netted him close to $1.5 billion.

So if he doesn't believe that success can teach you lessons, how is it that he has managed to succeed more than once and become a billionaire? "We do enough self-analysis to know what the components of our model are, and we exercise discipline to adhere to that model. But I can't tell you which of these are critical components," he says.

"Which of them could be relaxed to obtain the same or a better result, I'm not sure."

In my universe I might put it like this: If it ain't broke, don't fix it.

R. J. Kirk's Best Mistake, in His Own Words

My business consists of organizing teams of people to produce successful results. This is the unifying theme.

I'm like Louis B. Mayer or David O. Selznick. I'm a good executive producer. I don't know a lot about acting, or lighting, or costumes, or directing, but I'm pretty good at determining who *does* know about those things and figuring out which groups of those could work together toward an end point that I have established in my mind.

My best mistake relates to a time in my career when I had already produced a number of minor successes. By that time I had been doing transactions with a number of pharmaceutical companies. My original business was a specialty distributor. That cast me in the role of chief of business development for the specialty distributor. And I found myself in negotiation with the world's largest pharmaceutical and then biotherapeutic companies to obtain the right to distribute those products in the physician office marketplace.

Q.   Which company was this?

General Injectables & Vaccines.

I had experienced the following several times: I would be in negotiation with the business development person of a major company, and this fellow and I might be hitting it off and maybe the deal sounded like it might make sense, and it would be getting traction on both sides. And this fellow let it be known to me that he was available for employment, and would sometimes actually proffer his resume. I thought that the topic, every time this happened, was improper while this business discussion was going on. So I always deferred discussion about this while a transaction was in the air.

But in truth, after the deal, and without any prearrangement, I usually thought well of the people with whom I had satisfactory business dealings. And knowing that these people *were* available I would sometimes hire them. Now this is after the transaction. I do not believe I ever did anything improper.

If you've done satisfactory business with someone, you usually have a favorable impression of the other guy. My suggestion is that many times that favorable impression is based on vanity. In other words, the other guy liked your deal; the other guy liked you; therefore, you think that he must be pretty good. So my suggestion in terms of what I learned is that ain't necessarily so!

And this is how I learned it.

At a time when I had collected four such people—three in the means I just described, and one to obtain the approval of a major shareholder of the company that I was running; in other words, he was a relative of a major shareholder (which also is a wrong reason to hire someone!).

So I ended up with four of these people in my employ. And at a certain point, they betrayed me en masse.

Here's the lesson. I was furious at them for about two seconds. And in the third second or so I realized that I should have expected this. I really had no independent basis of belief that these individuals were loyal to me.

My supposition had been that while they had not been the most loyal individuals in the past, most certainly they would be loyal to me. And again, my suggestion is that that belief was born mostly out of my own vanity.

Maybe they make themselves available to you. But that's enough to put you on notice. And the fact that they liked you shouldn't be taken as something that is probative of their good judgment.

The truth is, with respect to all four of these individuals, that I never trusted them. And eventually I found that I should never have acted as if I did.

Q.   There must have been some business event in which they took another side.

I had a few occasions of this type in which it seemed to me that they were really doing more advocacy for the counterparties in our transactions. So I found myself scrutinizing their work much more than I should have felt the need to.

And then ultimately they resigned en masse to start their own company, which they had been working on for months, as we later learned—while they were employed by my company (GIV Holdings).

Q.   Does their company still exist?

No, they went out of business.

Q.   Do you get some pleasure in that?

Oh, it's better than that actually. These fellows sued me. I give profits interests in all the things that we are doing to all of our executives. And I had given these gentlemen such profits interests. We were in the middle of a transaction, and without going in to all the details, they sued me related to that.

I did have satisfaction because I will tell you I settled with these gentlemen their completely meritless lawsuit by buying securities from them for 50 cents a share that would later turn into New River Pharmaceuticals, which would, in a few years, sell to Shire for a split-adjusted $128 a share. They got the 50 cents a share that they sued to obtain!

I know that their business did fail, but beyond that I don't know where they are.

Q.   You didn't have that experience with others whom you employed in more conventional ways?

Never. I recognized that the core members of the team really are co-venturers in every sense of the word. They believe in what we're doing. They're not working on other things, they are completely loyal, and I am completely loyal to them.

In fact, the reason I had the loyalty to the others was that I had granted it to them.

I really do believe that I am the one who committed the error—or at least the error for which I'm responsible—and there was this dynamic of distrust that pervaded those relationships ab initio [from the beginning].

Q.   Did you have a gut feeling about this?

Yes. There was an element of distrust that pervaded these relationships. And by the way, I see this quite often in business.

If you want loyalty, you have to grant loyalty. People are not loyal to an organization simply because an organization hired them and pays them regularly. It doesn't work that way.

I always distrusted them.

It was not possible for me to claim or expect their trust, because I had never trusted them. The reason I had never trusted them was because of the situation that had originally occurred when each of them—in three cases—had communicated his availability for employment. And therefore I never trusted them.

About R. J. Kirk

Randal J. Kirk founded Third Security, LLC in March 1999 and has served as its chief executive officer since that time. In 1984, he co-founded General Injectables & Vaccines, Inc. and served as chairman of the board prior to the 1998 sale of the company. Mr. Kirk also co-founded King Pharmaceuticals, Inc. in 1993. Additionally, in 1996 he founded and became chairman of the board of New River Pharmaceuticals, Inc. (previously traded on NASDAQ prior to its acquisition by Shire plc in 2007) and was president and chief executive officer between October 2001 and April 2007.

Mr. Kirk has served as a member of the board of directors of Clinical Data, Inc. since 2002 and as chairman of the board since 2004; as a member of the board of directors of Halozyme Therapeutics, Inc. (NASDAQ: HALO) since May 2007; as chairman of the board of directors of Intrexon Corporation since February 2008; and as chairman of the board of directors of Cyntellect, Inc. since September 2008. He served as a member of the board of directors of Scios, Inc. (previously traded on NASDAQ prior to its acquisition by Johnson & Johnson) between February 2000 and May 2002.

In 2009, Virginia Governor Timothy M. Kaine appointed Mr. Kirk to serve on the University of Virginia's Board of Visitors. Prior to that honor, he served as rector of the Radford University Board of Visitors and also on the University's Foundation Board. In July 2006, Mr. Kirk was chosen by the governor to sit on the Virginia Advisory Council on Revenue Estimates. A year later, he accepted a position on the board of directors for the Virginia University Research Partnership.

Mr. Kirk began his professional career in the private practice of law. He holds a BA in business from Radford University and a JD from the University of Virginia.

Third Security, LLC's story began in the early 1980s, when its founder, R. J. Kirk, was a young attorney in southwest Virginia. From his initial investments, including the formation of General Injectables & Vaccines, Inc.

(GIV) in 1984, Mr. Kirk quickly distilled the principles that became the foundation of Third Security's management model.

GIV was sold to a major competitor for more than $67 million in 1998; and shortly thereafter, Mr. Kirk and a handful of associates launched Third Security in 1999 to help manage their personal investments and affiliated entities. Their investments included a company that became New River Pharmaceuticals, Inc., which went public in 2004 and was sold to a British concern for $2.6 billion in early 2007. Today, Third Security has more than 50 employees.

Part Three
The Next Generation

I t's a challenge to find someone old enough to have achieved a level of notable success but young enough to represent the next wave of business leaders. But those are the folks who have been gracious enough to participate in this part of the book.

Business leadership is proven over time, and these subjects are well on their way to firming up their credentials and reputations. It is probably just a matter of time before they take the reins of leadership from the legends and gurus who preceded them.

I must confess that the naming of this section has more than a little to do with my long-standing respect for Jean-Luc Picard, the captain of the Starship *Enterprise* in *Star Trek: The Next Generation*. He possesses numerous traits that make for a classic leader. He displays nobility and strength, as well as compassion and grace under pressure, and executes decisions with certainty and the utmost concern for the members of his crew. And if you ever meet me and bring up the fact that he's a fictional character, I will change the subject on you.

The reality is that the people in this section tend to be younger than most of the other participants in this book. But they've managed to attract acclaim within their fields of expertise even though they may not have reached a widespread notice or household awareness that will likely come.

Prepare to read the section. *Engage.*

Chapter 18

MEREDITH WHITNEY

Bank analyst, predicted mortgage problems and financial fallout

In 2009, on *Time* magazine's list of 100 "World's Most Influential People"

One of the *Wall Street Journal*'s 50 Women to Watch

M eredith Whitney is disarming. She looks you straight in the eye and states her points so clearly and simply that the content is emphasized and the style of the delivery is minimized. You keep waiting for her to add a huge inflection to emphasize a point, something to match the impact of what she's saying. But with Meredith, it's the content that matters, not the show.

Which is not to say her words don't pack a punch; they do. Like when she made "the call" on October 31, 2007. As a bank analyst at Oppenheimer she predicted that Citigroup would raise capital, sell assets, or cut its dividend. The company's stock plummeted and the financial crisis ensued. It was almost as if she was the only analyst who had the guts to say, as the never-ending parade of financial institutions wreaked havoc on Wall Street and Main Street, "The emperor has no clothes!"

Her stock soared.

The *New York Post* has called her one of the 50 Most Powerful Women in New York City. In 2007 she was listed as the second best stock picker in the capital market industry on Forbes.com's "The Best Analysts: Stock Pickers." Her extremely bearish view on banks landed her on the cover of the August 18, 2008, issue of *Fortune* magazine. In October 2008, she was ranked as one of the Fortune 500's "50 Most Powerful Women in Business." In 2008 she was named CNBC's "Power Player of the Year."

Impressed? Forget all that. Let me tell you what makes Meredith Whitney special.

I had the pleasure of working with Meredith from time to time when I was anchoring on a cable network. I won't tell you which network it was, but it rhymes with "docs."

At the time, the Iraq war was going on, and as a news anchor I would do a lot of interviews with experts on the Middle East. At some point in our shows, Meredith would come on and talk about what was going on in the business world. She was excellent: affable, well informed, and an easy interview.

One day in the greenroom before a show we were talking about various issues going on in the world, and she asked me if there were a couple of books I would recommend on the Middle East.

Think about that. Here she was, a Brown-educated woman who had worked at Oppenheimer and had been the head of financial institution research at Wachovia. She was a television regular on the major cable networks, someone who would soon return to Oppenheimer to cover banks and brokerages. She knew more about banks and assessing the strength or weakness of a balance sheet or business endeavor than I would ever know.

Why does she need to know about the Middle East?

Because she's curious. Because she wants to understand something better. Because she's willing to say, even out loud and in public, "I don't know enough about this" in order to become better informed about it.

That is somebody born to be an analyst. More than that, this is someone you can trust.

And really, isn't that what doomed Wall Street—a violation of trust?

It has been said that Meredith Whitney can move the markets. That kind of power can come and go. But she has established that whatever her analysis, she calls them as she sees them. You can trust her. That's why she can look you right in the eye.

"As you go through your career," Meredith tells me, "you get a lot more confidence in your gut—because you *are* effectively who you are. So once you allow your personality to truly come out, then I think you can really excel at your job."

That's a lesson that she learned by following her gut, even when it was hard to do.

Meredith Whitney's Best Mistake, in Her Own Words

At 28 years old I was offered the job to build and run the financial institutions research effort at First Union, which became Wachovia. I was the youngest person on the Street to be offered to do that. Moving into the role at 28 was daunting. Very few of my friends had that serious a job. It was hard for many reasons, but I knew it was the right thing to do at the time.

I was there from fall of 1998 to May of 2002. During that time, I did what I set out to do, which was to build a financial institutions practice. I really called the financials right—bullish at the right time, which was the break after the dot-com bust in March of 2001. I went very bullish on the financials with the idea that so many stocks were getting discounted because of their *lack* of cash flow earnings, financials with strong cash flows should therefore garner a premium multiple and capital flows. I believed that with a lot of the credit card names, and other companies that had strong cash flow, earnings would outperform—and they did.

I got progressively bearish in early 2002, which was the right call.

So all that time I was very pleased with the progress I was making professionally, but I didn't get the type of feedback or response that I wanted from management. I was passed over for managing director in 2001. It hurt my feelings—I don't mind saying that—because I was such a strong producer. I was one of their top-producing analysts, if not *the* top, in the department.

The first time it happened I was ready to quit on the spot. But while I was in the process of quitting, they offered a third year on my two-year contract, for more money. I was very uncertain about it, but it was right after the dot-com crash—things were getting tougher and I was advised by many to take the safe route. So I took the deal.

But I just didn't like the place anymore—they hadn't given me a full vote of confidence. It wasn't about the money. I always expected to be one of those happy employees of the month types! All I wanted was acknowledgment.

 So I went through a year, got paid, and—wasn't promoted again! At that point I was heartbroken to work for a place that wasn't acknowledging me. So I ended up quitting.

This was a mistake in this sense: By quitting, I could get my pay that was in the form of restricted stock, but since part of my contract also included forgivable loans, I actually had to *pay* the firm to leave. Then there was the idea, oh, if you leave Wall Street, are you ever going to get another job? And I had to sign a three-year noncompete agreement to get out of my deal with them. So it may have looked like a mistake, but I left the position based on my gut.

And it was the greatest mistake I ever made!

I ended up taking two and a half years away from the business, although I hated every minute of it in the sense that I'm a worker—I can get a thousand things done in a day if I'm chockablock busy, but if I have too much time on my hands I'm significantly less productive. Not working drives me crazy. Plus, it took me out of the business at a time that the market was starting to rally, in 2003.

But during that time I read a ton, I traveled—I got perspective—and most importantly I met my husband. I don't think that as grizzled as I was, working at the pace I was working, I would have had the chance to slow down enough and meet someone.

So for me, it was the best mistake I ever made, because being out of the system, I was even more independent when I came back. Being with my husband left me even more independent because his life was so different. I'd go home and Wall Street wasn't the center of the universe.

When I tried to get back into the workforce, everyone assumed I must have been fired. And it couldn't have been further from the case. The day after I left I was named one of the *Wall Street Journal*'s top stock pickers in my category. At the time I was actually leaving at the top of my career!

So coming back into the business, I had to start at the bottom again. Three years is a long time to be away from the business, so I had to reestablish myself from scratch. But I had over a decade's worth of experience on the Street, so I could be quick and outmaneuver people.

In January or February of 2006, I went hyper bullish on the brokers, which was a contrarian position. I think Goldman Sachs was at $140 and I put a $190 price target on it—people thought I was crazy—and the stock ended up over $200 that year.

People had no, or low, expectations of me, so I was below their radar until all of a sudden I wasn't. And meanwhile I had so much more experience than so much of my competition, but I had been away—so it was perfect because you always want to be underestimated.

 I had to work really hard to establish myself, and what I brought was an unorthodox, unconventional approach to research that was unique. And that was all my gut. I let my gut drive me with so much of my research and use the data to prove or disprove my gut. I never expect things to be the same forever.

Having success by following your gut gives you confidence to really trust it.

But then I left CIBC because the culture wasn't what I was looking for. So my gut was that I should go start one that is reflective of that. I've only been with two firms in my career. Well, three actually. I'll be with this one [Meredith Whitney Advisory Group, LLC] for the duration!

About Meredith Whitney

Meredith Whitney is the CEO of Meredith Whitney Advisory Group, LLC, a macro and strategy-driven investment research firm. Well followed for her core research, Ms. Whitney and her team also focus on a broad section of financials, including large, small, and midsize banks, brokers, and independent commercial and consumer finance companies.

Prior to founding Meredith Whitney Advisory Group, Ms. Whitney was a managing director and senior financial institutions analyst for Oppenheimer & Company, Inc. Throughout her tenure at Oppenheimer, she was most noted for her research on the ultimate decline in home prices, the future of the U.S. mortgage industry, and the consumer lending market, including specific focus on the credit card industry.

In 2007, she wrote prolifically on the threats surrounding the weighted influence of the rating agencies on regulatory capital determinants and the risks of the monoline insurers on financial institutions. In 2006, she presented to the Federal Deposit Insurance Corporation (FDIC) on the U.S. consumer and the risks in the subprime market.

Previously, Ms. Whitney worked as a financial analyst at Wachovia Securities, CIBC World Markets, and Oppenheimer.

In 2009, Ms. Whitney was named as one of *Time* magazine's list of 100 "World's Most Influential People" and was ranked the #1 investment analyst in her category by the *Wall Street Journal*. Also in 2009, she was named one of *Fortune*'s Top 50 Most Powerful Women for the second consecutive year, and Crain's 40 under 40. In 2008, she was named in the *Wall Street Journal*'s 50 Women to Watch and *Smart Money*'s Power 30. She was also ranked in *Institutional Investor*'s 2008 All-American Research Team. Ms. Whitney graduated with honors from Brown University. She currently serves on the board of trustees of the Lawrenceville School.

Chapter 19

JASON KILAR

CEO of Hulu LLC

Graduate of Harvard Business School

Almost 10 years in management at Amazon.com

I have seen the future of television, and it is Hulu.

Well, maybe not Hulu precisely, but something a lot like it. There's no question that when you go to Hulu.com, you're getting a glimpse into the future where television and the Internet are brought together.

You can watch thousands of popular (and not so popular) TV shows at the web site—free of charge for a certain period of time. Did you miss Jon Stewart's *Daily Show*? Want to see what *The View* had to say the other day? Did you miss *Ugly Betty* or *Desperate Housewives*?

Don't TiVo it—Hulu it!

You can also pay a premium for access to a library of previously aired shows and content you might not find anywhere else. And remember, these are professionally produced shows—this isn't YouTube.

At Hulu, you get the feeling that the fading line between television and computer is vanishing completely. As a consumer of entertainment, do you just want to punch a few buttons and make the show appear magically on a screen? This is pretty close.

Here's how CEO Jason Kilar describes his company.

"Hulu is an online premium video service, a way for people to find and enjoy the world's premium content when, where, and how they want to."

Doesn't that sound like an appropriate and proper statement from a Harvard Business School grad with a degree from the University of North Carolina?

It should. Kilar has the right pedigree from an educational standpoint to go far in the entertainment industry. And his business experience includes working for the Walt Disney Company for two years and Amazon.com for over nine years. That's what it takes for NBC, Fox, and ABC to trust you to run a web site that could hold a clue to answering the question that is vexing all media companies: What business model will allow a profit when you've spent millions on content and nobody wants to pay for it?

"There is a world full of fantastic content creators. We work with them to distribute and help that content find a large, disposable audience," he says. And part of Kilar's job at Hulu is to take the content that has been created through decades of old media distribution and make it accessible to those in the present. But he also looks to the future:

We are entering what I believe is a golden age of media. We provide the ability to find and discover the world's premium content when, where, and how you want to. That happens to be our mission statement.

But what does a guy who ran the DVD business for Amazon know about providing media content online?

"On the surface they're very different industries," Kilar observes. "One is an advertising-supported industry and the other is a retail, cash-register-oriented industry. But there are so many similarities among disparate industries that most people don't see initially. Any company's success is largely a function of its culture." He notes:

You'll find that world-class companies have very common traits in regard to culture. So in regard to Hulu, one of the most important traits of our culture is that we are obsessive about our customers.

"Not surprisingly," he continues, "that is very similar to some of the world-class companies out there. Whether it's Amazon, Wal-Mart, Starbucks, you name it, there's this obsession about the customer and the customer experience. And we certainly aspire to be a world-class company. We know that we're just getting started and we haven't earned that yet, but that's what our aspiration is."

It just happens to be that our product is digital, while the Amazon product for the most part is physical, but that's a distinction that we don't get hung up on.

And, Kilar says, there are similarities from a very practical standpoint. "We both have a tremendous log of items to present to users, and we want to make sure that people can discover them—that they can search and find them, that they can have a wonderful customer experience around those products. When you think about the larger things that matter, which are culture and values and principles, and the way that we do things online, there are a lot of similarities."

But if Kilar is right, that companies are more about guiding values than what they sell, where did he learn the appropriate values to drive Hulu? At Amazon.com, where the company's CEO, Jeff Bezos, taught him lessons on leadership through the good times and during crises. Kilar says:

You learn more through failure and tough times than you do through good times.

And it was a particular event that occurred while Kilar was at Amazon that stays with him even to this day.

Jason Kilar's Best Mistake, in His Own Words

This happened while I was at Amazon. There was a time I was running the DVD business. It was November of 1998, and business was doing very well. And we wanted to analytically determine how low we could drop prices on our DVDs.

So the vision of Amazon was, in addition to having the biggest selection, to also offer great value for the products offered on Amazon.

What my team endeavored to do was figure this out analytically: Could we afford to lower prices further than we already had?

The way we went about that was to try to do a very scientific test. We pride ourselves on being very rigorous analytically. To the degree that we could observe data to help influence our decisions, that's what we aspired to do here as well.

We embarked on a three-week test online in our DVD and video store where our prices had already been cut for a long period of time.

 What we tried to do for three weeks was to lower the prices for half the audience over a 21-day period. It was all done randomly because we wanted to see after three weeks of testing how much more demand we could drive with lower prices.

If enough people bought more DVDs, we could justify lowering the prices because at the end of the day you have to sell a lot more DVDs if you're selling them for a lower price than you were before. So it was a very simple math exercise.

I think you can imagine where this went. We went live with the test. At some point during that period somebody basically wrote something online saying, "Hey, there's something interesting here. I got this price for the DVD, but my friend is getting a price of this amount for the same DVD."

What happened was an old-fashioned you-know-what storm. This blew up for us rather quickly up in Seattle. There were a lot of theories out there about what we were doing. There were a lot of accusations that we were doing things specifically for people who had purchased a lot from us before, or that we were doing something for new customers only, or we were doing something based on economic information that we had no access to. . . .

So there were a whole lot of conspiracy theories about "What is Amazon up to?"

The minute this started heading in that direction we clearly had to assemble a war room.

 This was a mistake on my part, for going off and doing this test the way we executed it. It was well intentioned, but clearly not the right thing for reasons that are painfully obvious in hindsight.

What was interesting about this was that the war room was myself, the head of PR, the head of communications, and Jeff Bezos, the CEO of the company.

We were in the sixth-floor conference room at the Amazon headquarters, and out front were a number of news trucks, with their satellite antennas up, and everybody was reporting live from Amazon headquarters and wanted to understand what our comments were on this topic.

What was so interesting was how Jeff handled me, number one, and second, the situation. You can sort of imagine how I felt walking up there, going up the stairs to tell them what had happened, and what we were doing about it.

I wasn't feeling too good about my career in that situation. At the time I had been with the company about two years, and I was very excited about where the company was going, but I had a lot on my hands about the PR and the disorder of the company.

 As I walked into the conference room, I was struck by how calm and cool Jeff Bezos was. You could just look down through the window and see all these satellite trucks, but how calm and cool he was! He was clearly focused on the matter at hand, but he was extremely calm, even relaxed in terms of how he interacted with me.

He was serious in regard to the topic, but relaxed in terms of the interpersonal interaction. And he was supportive of me personally.

So we separated the topics from the people. He did that, quite frankly. And it was just very interesting that we very quickly got to the root of the problem. And that was that perception was as important and valuable here as actual integrity in terms of how we operated. One of the most important principles at Amazon is the scientific approach to the business. It is certainly near and dear to everyone's heart at that company. It's something I've always been inspired by in terms of companies I've wanted to be associated with. And it's certainly something that we do here at Hulu in terms of taking the high road on everything that we do.

It was very clear that this was well intentioned but in hindsight a very big mistake because the perception of Amazon as approaching things in a high-integrity way clearly outweighed what our intent was.

So we stopped doing the test immediately.

 The second common theme here was that I learned through this process that both companies and individuals are defined most during periods of crisis. In terms of how Amazon was defined and how Jeff Bezos was defined in this case, he reinforced and confirmed our high-integrity approach to business.

That was critical for Amazon as a company and critical for all of us as individuals. He was so interested in that teaching moment to help guide and support someone he was focused on in that meeting.

So for me it was very transformative and very reaffirming in terms of how great leaders (like Jeff Bezos) act.

And keep in mind, this is a guy who knew that he was going to be woken at 3 A.M. that next morning and go on the *Today* show to present an apology to the country about what we did and what we learned from it and how we were going to proceed forward. So he knew that was in his future, going on to get grilled by a major news anchor. And immediately he wanted to do the right thing, which was to apologize, and explain what had happened. He would say we were well intentioned, but we clearly made a mistake, and here's what we were going to do going forward.

 In hindsight, though incredibly painful—and it would have been nice to have avoided that—I learned so much as a leader as an individual, and I learned a lot about companies and what defines companies. And oftentimes companies are defined in periods of great crises.

Q.   So about the test itself—did you learn anything from it?

It did not affect sales overall because it was a relatively quick test. We did end up lowering prices. In a long-term way, sales went up a lot. I think lowering prices had a good bit to do with it; it wasn't the only reason, but it was part of the reason. The short answer is that we ended up lowering prices and Amazon continues to do that. So that was a helpful moment for the company for business reasons as well, to put a heavier focus on the price side of the equation.

Somewhere around 2000, we implemented Super Saver shipping, which is as long as you spent $25 or more, you would get free shipping. That was a price-lowering strategy. In the short term, that cost Amazon a tremendous amount of bottom-line money because you were getting $4, $5, $6 of shipping revenue, and the next day you are not. And your costs are still there whether it's the post office, FedEx, or UPS. But in the long-term business, Amazon grew so much more aggressively because of that price-lowering strategy. Ultimately there was more bottom-line impact for the company. So you have to be brave and long term focused when it comes to lowering prices. And yes, in the end, lowering prices in the DVD store was the right thing to do for both the top line and the bottom line.

About Jason Kilar

Jason Kilar serves as the CEO of Hulu, an online video joint venture of News Corporation, NBC Universal, Walt Disney Company, and Providence Equity

Partners. Jason joined Hulu after nearly a decade of experience at Amazon
.com, where he served in a variety of key leadership roles. After writing the
original business plan for Amazon's entry into the video and DVD businesses, he ultimately became vice president and general manager of Amazon's
North American media businesses, which included the company's books,
music, video, and DVD categories. He later served as senior vice president,
worldwide application software, where he led an organization of hundreds
of world-class technologists and reported directly to CEO Jeff Bezos. Jason
began his career with the Walt Disney Company, where he worked for Disney
Design & Development. He received his MBA from Harvard Business School
and graduated Phi Beta Kappa from the University of North Carolina, Chapel
Hill, where he studied business administration, and journalism and mass
communication.

Chapter 20

IAN BREMMER

Founded global political risk research and consulting firm Eurasia Group

Created first global political risk index

Author of several books, including *The End of the Free Market: Who Wins the War between States and Corporations?*

an Bremmer looks young for his age of 40. But he has always looked young compared to those around him. Like when he went to Tulane University on an academic scholarship. Of course, he was only 15 then. And he was younger than the other teachers at Stanford University when he got his PhD at 24.

But what strikes you about Ian is not how young he looks, but how wise he sounds, and how easily he can talk about world issues, whether it's on NPR, CNBC, or across the table at brunch at one of his favorite quaint restaurants in Washington, D.C., where I last saw him in person.

As he talks about the most complicated financial issues, drawing from his travels around the world and his one-on-one discussions with top global political and business leaders, the course of conversation flows as breezily as if he's talking about who's going to win the next U.S. Open tennis tournament.

But you suddenly realize he's talking about something like the political shifts going on in Uzbekistan, or the undercurrent of generational unease in Saudi Arabia. He makes *you* feel smart simply because you can digest what he's saying so readily. But don't be fooled. This is someone who not only knows from personal experience what's going on around the world, but also has the book learning that would put you to shame all by itself.

In fact, he gave up a bright, cushy future as a professor at Stanford University in order to start his own private-sector political consulting company, Eurasia Group. He explains:

> I was too young. The idea of sitting in a beautiful office and thinking glorious thoughts is fine when you've had a great life and you're 60. But when you're 24 and you're entrepreneurial, if you want to accomplish something, if you think that you can actually make a difference in the world, you can't sit. You've got too much wound-up energy.

Eurasia Group now has research analysts throughout the world in order to assess the political and financial risk of investing in roughly 80 countries. He provides the research to Wall Street and inside the Beltway, and to multinational corporations. (He maintains homes in New York and Washington, with offices in both of those locations as well as in London.) Through his company he feels he has more of an effect on the world than if he had stayed in the comfortable confines of academia.

"Without wanting to criticize 90 percent of the people who are actually teaching, the fact was when I was 24, I felt like a fraud. If I were going to go and declare my unabashed expertise and be able to mold young minds, I'd better teach them about the way the world really works. But I don't think I knew very much about how the world really works, but you can pretend that you do when you're in that milieu."

Ian Bremmer's Best Mistake, in His Own Words

When you get a full scholarship to go to one of the best schools to get your PhD, you're told that you're a success only if you become an academic. You become an academic at the best school and you teach—you devote your life to the academy.

I think that's a mistake. I didn't know it at the time. And the best mistake I ever made is that I listened to those people. So when I finished my PhD I was convinced I should be an academic.

I got into that and I did the research and I started doing the teaching. And you really hole yourself up. You go into the stacks and you do your research and you take all your book knowledge and you pass it on to the students.

Being in front of a classroom of people that are very smart, roughly your age—frankly, some of them are older—when you have no experience, when you've done nothing, you've not seen the world, then you can't have pride in your knowledge.

I may have been entertaining, but I don't think I had much to offer. And I think it gave me a great sense of how important it was to apply knowledge.

 Their parents were paying $30,000 a year to send them to Stanford to hear from somebody—a lot of somebodies, frankly—that had never really done anything in the real world.

After you finish a lecture, after you finish the course, you see what's happening in the world. These things actually matter to people's lives. I mean, these things are happening in the real world. You're talking about political context. The realization comes over a period of time that you don't really have the ability to make a connection with that.

For instance, you have genocide in Darfur, but you have no way of describing that because you haven't been there; you haven't lived through it. You have high-level negotiations in a summit, but you haven't been to a summit, so you don't know what a summit's like.

Whether it's talks on proliferation, whether it's ethnic conflict, whether it's European Union accession talks, you've never been involved in any of those things.

And also you've never been responsible for analyzing them and then being accountable for whether you're right or wrong.

What the PhD learns is how to hedge, because you have to be right all the time. And the only way to be right all the time is if you can never really be wrong.

So typically when you're asked what's going to happen, you hedge. You don't really want to say, because you don't really want accountability of that research being wrong.

 If you're in the markets, if you're a businessman, you don't have the luxury of being able to hedge. You can do it when you're giving a speech, but you can't do it when you're making a decision. And in the real world, decisions have to be made.

I guess the real thing is when you're an academic you don't have to make decisions. But when you want to teach people about how decisions are made, you have to have made decisions yourself. I think it's critical.

Q. So you started Eurasia Group, a global political risk research and consulting firm. Do you feel like you're making a difference now?

Yes. The world is changing too fast for me to try making a difference one person at a time. Because the best academics, that's what they do. They make a major difference in individual students' lives. And over time, that has a trickle-down effect and before you know it it's been a generation and it makes a big difference.

 But if you want to understand international politics, it strikes me that you're going to learn the most from people who have in some way been practitioners. There aren't many policy people who have actually been in the private sector. I like to think I'm now one of them.

About Ian Bremmer

Ian Bremmer is the president of Eurasia Group, the leading global political risk research and consulting firm.

In 1998, Bremmer founded Eurasia Group with just $25,000. Today, the company has offices in New York, Washington, and London, as well as a network of experts and resources around the world. Eurasia Group provides financial, corporate, and government clients with information and insight on how political developments move markets.

Bremmer created Wall Street's first global political risk index, and is the author of several books, including *The J Curve: A New Way to Understand Why Nations Rise and Fall* (Simon & Schuster, 2006), which was selected by the *Economist* as one of the best books of 2006, and *The Fat Tail: The Power of Political Knowledge for Strategic Investing* (Oxford University Press, 2009). His latest book, *The End of the Free Market: Who Wins the War between States and Corporations?* (Portfolio, May 2010), details the new global phenomenon of state capitalism and its geopolitical implications. Bremmer is also a frequent writer and commentator in the media. He writes "The Call" blog on ForeignPolicy .com and is a contributor for the *Wall Street Journal*; he has also published articles in the *Washington Post*, the *New York Times*, *Newsweek*, *Harvard Business Review*, and *Foreign Affairs*. He is a panelist for CNN International's *Connect the World* and appears regularly on CNBC, Fox News Channel, National Public Radio, and other networks.

Bremmer has a PhD in political science from Stanford University (1994), and was the youngest-ever national fellow at the Hoover Institution. At present he teaches at Columbia University, and he has held faculty positions at the EastWest Institute and the World Policy Institute. In 2007, he was named a Young Global Leader of the World Economic Forum. His analysis focuses on global macro political trends and emerging markets, which he defines as "those countries where politics matter at least as much as economics for market outcomes."

Chapter 21

JIM BUCKMASTER

CEO of Craigslist

Architect of Craigslist home page design

Dropped out of the University of Michigan Medical School

Jim Buckmaster responded to an ad on Craigslist looking for a programmer. The job was at Craigslist itself. Not only did he get the job, but 11 months later he was *running* Craigslist. That just might be the Internet equivalent of working your way up the corporate ladder by starting in the mailroom.

Of course, to call Craigslist "corporate" would be a stretch. Sure, the web site gets an estimated 50 million unique visits a month in the United States alone, and an estimated 20 billion page views worldwide, ranking it in the top 10 in the United States and top 22 globally [wiki per Compete.com on April 7, 2009]. But it is run by a mere couple dozen or so employees who cling to their goal of serving their clients' needs, not Wall Street's or Silicon Valley's expectations. Buckmaster says:

> A lot of people over the years see our approach as being weird or unorthodox, but that doesn't mean that we've felt the pressure to conform to the way everyone else approaches running an Internet enterprise.

What is weird or unorthodox? Certainly not the concept. Described simply, Craigslist is a web site where classified ads are posted. But it is more than that. It's an online community with an attitude. The site touts its "relatively non-commercial nature, public service mission, and non-corporate culture."

Visiting the Craigslist site at www.craigslist.org is like taking a trip back to the early days of Internet site development. If anything in the Internet world could be called old-school, this is it. The simple design, the absence of banner ads and other eye-catching images reminds you of a day in the mid-1990s when hooking up to the Internet involved a telephone modem and a fuzzy sound followed by a beep to indicate you're online and ready to go.

None of that is by coincidence. Buckmaster has had a hand in keeping the approach straightforward. Classified ads are simple, and that's what Craigslist tries to be. It lists more classified ads than any other medium in the world, an estimated 40 million new ones each month. It also lists more than a million job ads each month, making it a player in that arena as well. But you shouldn't be fooled by the simplicity of the site into thinking that this isn't a major business. It is, and newspapers across the country can tell you that Internet sites like Craigslist have played a significant role in the newspapers' collective financial demise.

By now a lot of people know the story. The site was launched in 1995 by its founder, Craig Newmark, who wanted to send his friends a list of events in the San Francisco area. The early postings—"Craigslist"—sent to e-mail addresses included many social events of interest to software and Internet developers. The number of postings and subscribers grew quickly, and the users found the new "Craigslist" a great way to communicate with a lot of people in an inexpensive way.

Postings began to include jobs, and later, housing, items for sale, services, discussion forums, and eventually a personals section. (Craigslist received some criticism for allowing "erotic services" listings, but in 2009 replaced them with an "adult services" section, which requires a fee and is policed by employees to prevent ads for prostitution.)

It creates revenue (as of January 2010) by charging for job ads in select cities: San Francisco, New York, Los Angeles, San Diego, Boston, Chicago, Washington, D.C., and Portland, Oregon. One of the benefits of charging for job ads is the upgrading of their quality, with the virtual elimination of get-rich-quick ads.

The multicity architecture now includes more than 500 cities worldwide. It was implemented by Buckmaster when he came to the company, situated in

Newmark's San Francisco apartment, in January 2000. As lead programmer, he designed the home page and helped round out the online community with a search engine, discussion forums, a self-posting process, and a flagging system. In November of the same year, he became Craigslist's CEO.

Despite the enormous success of the Craigslist brand, Buckmaster and Newmark have resisted outside pressure to monetize the company's value by doing things like charging for *all* of its ads—most are still free—and going public in order to bring in millions of dollars to help fund the company's expansion and create an enormous payoff for its owners. But Buckmaster and Newmark, as the primary owners (eBay owns roughly 25 percent, bought from a former employee), have shown no inclination to turn the perceived Craigslist value into gigantic bank accounts.

Yet Buckmaster's own bio on Craigslist proudly touts arrows that have come his way: "Possibly the only CEO ever described as anti-establishment, a communist, and a socialistic anarchist. . . ." The latter charge was lodged by Martin Sorrell—that's *Sir* Martin Sorrell—the chief executive at WPP Group, one of the largest advertising companies in the world.

The Craigslist web site links to Sorrell's 2006 quote (FinancialTimes.com, June 20, 2006):

"How do you deal with socialistic anarchists?" he [Sorrell] asked, referring to Craigslist, the popular, free classified advertising site that has been threatening revenues at U.S. city newspapers.

"The Internet is the most socialistic force you've ever seen," he added, noting that the response from some media groups had been to offer their content for free in traditional and digital form.

"They have decided—'if I don't eat my children, somebody else will,'" he told executives from UK regional newspapers attending an industry conference, adding that he disapproved of giving away content for free. "You should charge for it if the consumer values the content," he said.

But change in the newspaper business model was inevitable when the dot-com era arrived. The traditional model included selling classified ads and display ads, and charging subscribers for purchasing the publication. The reason that a reader could buy a paper for just a quarter at the vending machine was that the primary profit generator was the ads. But the Internet has destroyed that profit-making model.

As Buckmaster says, "There's been a sea change in underlying technologies and a lot of newspapers have had trouble adapting to that sea change."

Warren Buffett may have put it best in an interview on CNBC on May 4, 2009. He argued that if the Internet had existed before newspapers, newspapers would never have made it. "[If] I came along one day and said I have got this wonderful idea: We are going to chop down some trees up in Canada and ship them to a paper mill, which will cost us a fortune to run through and deliver newsprint, and then we'll ship that down to some newspaper, and we'll have a whole bunch of people staying up all night writing up things, and then we'll send a bunch of kids out the next day all over town delivering this thing, and we are going to really wipe out the Internet with this, it ain't going to happen."

And certainly the multitude of outlets for keeping up on the news hasn't helped newspapers. People just don't read them like they used to. And that demand for news is what gave newspapers their raison d'être. With the decline of that demand, as Buffett says, "The old virtuous circle, where big readership draws a lot of ads, which in turn draw more readers, has broken down."

Buckmaster touts Craigslist's strength over newspapers. "The online medium has stupendous advantages compared to print for classifieds," he says. "We've tried to take advantage of those to provide something that users would really love, and users are certainly enjoying the online classified medium."

But that's not to say that Craigslist is a nonprofit organization, which some loyalists may believe. Buckmaster set the record straight in an interview with Telegraph.co.uk in London. "We are not so much anti-capitalist. . . . We're fortunate enough to have built a very healthy business, even though we haven't attempted to. All we have done is stop short of trying to become insanely wealthy. We have met billionaires, and it sounds funny but it's not necessarily a bed of roses to have that kind of money.

"People with that kind of wealth have to walk around with bodyguards. Their friends and extended families look at them in a way they wouldn't necessarily choose. Their life becomes about figuring out how to employ all that money either by philanthropy or other means. So we don't consider it that revolutionary to have stopped short of that."

Jim Buckmaster's Best Mistake, in His Own Words

My best mistake was choosing to drop out of medical school about halfway through. This was at the University of Michigan Medical School. I got about halfway through and I had the feeling that this wasn't for me.

This, despite the fact that I had so much invested in the process, both financially and in time and energy. And it certainly felt like a mistake at the time, and I had a lot of people telling me it was a mistake. And I felt like it was a mistake for years and years afterward. But ultimately I thank my lucky stars I made that mistake.

And my grades were good. I had mostly As. I was near the top of the class. Number one, I just did not enjoy the process. Increasingly I found that I wasn't enjoying the study of medicine. I found it kind of dull and boring. And the practical experiences I was having—I just had a hunch this isn't what I wanted to do with my life.

And it's such an all-consuming profession, and I felt that with these kinds of persistent doubts I needed step away from it, at least temporarily. So the shape of my initial decision was to take a year off.

And then I took another year off, and another year off. . . . And I just ended up never going back.

Q.   How long had you been in med school?

I had completed almost two years [of four] and I had racked up large student loans.

I didn't really see a way I was going to pay those loans off in a timely fashion. That's at least partly why it seemed like a mistake at the time. I didn't really have a plan B.

If you continue, the loans are not a problem, because certainly that's one of the better-paying professions. And at that point I had no inkling that there was something waiting for me that would eventually pass what was possible in the medical profession.

Q.   Was there a moment when it struck you that you couldn't do med school anymore?

I found the study of pharmacology stupefyingly boring. Most people liken it to attempting to memorize the phone book, just memorizing a huge number of disjointed facts.

Q.   How soon did you know you did the right thing?

I can remember almost 10 years after I dropped out thinking, "I can't think of a route to getting to a job that pays even $50,000 a year." I was still in debt, and had no real career prospects at that point.

Kind of out of boredom I started learning as much as I could about the Unix operating system, and then shell programming, just because the work I was doing on data entry and data processing was quite dull.

Q.   At what point did you finally believe you made the right decision?

As soon as I got into Web programming. I was hooked from the beginning.

I would sometimes sit in my chair working 18 hours at a time—and a short amount of sleep and that was my day. I found it so interesting, and I thought, "Oh my gosh!" Here was something coming out of the blue that was very interesting and fun to do. The higher-ups were very encouraging, so it wasn't long before I knew I was onto something.

When the Internet and the Web rolled around, I was in the right place at the right time.

I ended up on the front end of a terabyte-scale data archive at the University of Michigan. It was a primary data archive for the political and social scientists that all major universities subscribed to. Up to that point they had been distributing data on nine-track tapes in the mail.

Researchers were able to access and download data sets through this Web interface, and ultimately doing this analysis online. In retrospect, there weren't too many other places with the kind of level of opportunity for Web programming that existed there at the archive circa 1994–1995.

So the timing was right. There was certainly an element of good fortune there, as I think invariably there is.

I just loved Web programming from the get-go. It was strictly a self-taught thing. But the wonderful thing about Web programming is each web page you can see the source programming for it. You can teach yourself. In fact, many of our programmers at Craigslist are self-taught.

Q.   What was guiding you?

At a gut level I wanted to do this. Yes, I have a tremendous amount of debt that I don't know how I'm going to pay off. Yes, there was a lot of self-doubt there. Yes, I left one of the better-paying professions that a lot of people aspire to. But according to my experience and how I'm doing, med school doesn't seem like it's right for me.

Despite the fact that I don't have a plan B, and I don't know how I'm going to pay off this debt, and everyone around me is telling me this is a mistake, the inner voice, or gut feeling—that definitely was in play there.

Q. What lesson would you pass along to someone else?

One, trust your gut instinct.

When it comes to doing something as important as what you're going to spend the rest of your life doing, you need to respect your gut instinct.

Another one is that it doesn't matter what you've invested in something. What you've invested in the past is to some degree immaterial. What you're looking at is the future and where you want to place your investments in the future.

These lessons were learned the hard way, but the story had a happy ending.

Success was assured before I ended up at this particular company. Success was finding something that I loved to do.

About Jim Buckmaster

Possibly the only CEO ever described as anti-establishment, a communist, and a socialistic anarchist, since 2000 Jim has led Craigslist to be the most used classified ads in any medium, and one of world's most popular web sites, while maintaining its public service mission, noncorporate vibe, and staff of 20 or so.

Before devolving into management, Jim contributed Craigslist's home page design, multicity architecture, discussion forums, search engine, community moderation system, self-posting process, personals categories (including missed connections), and best-of-craigslist.

Prior to Craigslist, Jim directed Web development for Creditland (defunct) and Quantum. In 1994–1995, he built the terabyte-scale, database-driven Web interface at the Interuniversity Consortium for Political and Social Research (ICPSR) through which researchers worldwide access the primary data archive for the social sciences.

After graduating summa cum laude from Virginia Tech (biochemistry), Jim attended medical school, studied classics, and made tofu at the University of Michigan. Now, alas, it's mostly business reads for him.

Ridiculously tall, Jim has been the subject of feature stories in the *New York Times*, the *Wall Street Journal*, the *Financial Times*, *Fortune* magazine, *BusinessWeek*, the *Guardian*, the *Daily Telegraph*, the *Sunday Times*, and *SF Chronicle*, and has made dozens of television appearances, including being denounced on Fox News by the late Reverend Jerry Falwell.

Chapter 22
JOHN CAPPELLETTI

Heisman Trophy winner

Played in National Football League (NFL) for Los Angeles Rams and San Diego Chargers

Business owner, classic car enthusiast

I f you meet John Cappelletti and are old enough to remember who he is— he won't bring it up—you can suddenly find yourself feeling like a kid again. You can forget everything that has occurred in your life for the past 30 years and you're back in the 1970s, feeling something you haven't felt in years: admiration.

John observes, "People seem to want to remember you at a time in your life and in their life that was special to them, whether they were 15 or 50."

Why would people do that around John Cappelletti? Because not everybody can say they played football in college, went undefeated while winning the Orange Bowl, won the Heisman Trophy as the best football player in America, then went on to play in the National Football League for eight seasons.

But wait, there's more. When John was given the Heisman award, standing at the podium on the dais next to Vice President Gerald Ford, his acceptance speech brought tears to the eyes of many in the room as he recounted the everyday struggles of his brother Joey, who was dying of leukemia. The speech made such an impression that a book was written and a television movie made about John and his brother's life (*Something for Joey*, in 1977).

"It's amazing that after all these years," John says, "I still get letters from kids who are reading this book in fifth grade. A teacher will ask them to write a letter about what they felt and what they got out of it, and the class puts together the letters and packages them up and I'll get 30 letters from a fifth-grade class in Indiana somewhere. Even after all this time it's unbelievable the value that story has brought to other people."

No, John's life hasn't exactly been run-of-the-mill. But as appreciative as he is about all the unsolicited attention he receives, it still creates a bit of a challenge because of what people think when they meet him. He says:

I think the biggest misconception is that life is somehow different for people who played college or professional sports, that we don't have the same challenges and struggles as everyone else. We are perceived as if we were still in college or playing professionally. But we do age; we do have families; we do have the everyday battles of life in general.

And it might also surprise people that even in the sports world ability alone doesn't determine opportunity. You might even say that office politics can sometimes play a role there, too. John learned this himself just before attending Penn State on a football scholarship.

He was invited to play in a statewide All-Star game in his home state of Pennsylvania. "And we got correspondence that said that your starting positions will be based on how fast you run the mile.

"I ran the fastest mile of all the running backs. But because of nepotism, I never saw the offensive side of the field. The guy that jumped over me at running back was a kid that went to Notre Dame, and his father was the running back coach for the All-Star game. I only got in toward the very end of the game, to play linebacker. I did very well, but it was not a blessing because Penn State started looking at me as a linebacker and not a running back."

In fact, during his first two years at Penn State John was put at linebacker. He finally got a chance to prove he was a pretty fair running back in his junior year by running for more than a thousand yards. In his senior year he won the Heisman and led his team to an undefeated season. Not bad for a linebacker.

His playing days with the Los Angeles Rams and the San Diego Chargers are well behind him—which is fine with him because he doesn't live in the past. But he does exhibit a work ethic that makes him exceptional as a business-person as well. He tries to bring the professional attitude of not getting too high or too low in the sports world to his world as a business owner (after a number of investments, he now owns a classic car dealership in Southern California). He looks at the never-ending stream of problems as challenges he can handle.

"I walk in here in the morning, and sometimes even before I get to my office I have a half hour's worth of 'Hey, can you take a look at this? What do you think about this? Something happened over the weekend and we've got to deal with it.' It's just dealing with challenges, because if you viewed every-thing as a problem instead of a challenge, it would probably get to you after a while.

"But if you say, 'Okay, let's lay it out and take a look at it and figure out the best way to deal with it,' you're not going to burn yourself out. This is as opposed to 'Gee, what the heck can go wrong next?'" John concludes:

> I feel like I've been in business long enough to know that stuff's going to go wrong. It does every day. How do you fix it? How do you deal with it? How do you make it better?

He has learned the value of that positive attitude over the years in the business world, and he's learned a lesson about investing in a business from an experience that was reminiscent of something that happened in that pre–Penn State All-Star game. But if you bring it up in conversation, he'll probably try to change the subject. He doesn't live in the past. He's dealing with the challenges of today.

John Cappelletti's Best Mistake, in His Own Words

In 2005 I was in partnership with fellow—we had gotten in business together, bought a building together, and worked the business for about three years—when unexpectedly he passed away.

He had a son there who worked the business, too. So for several more years I worked with the son. I was a minority partner in that business, owning something like 30 percent. I was also a minority partner in the building, because the three of us had owned it—the father, the son, and myself.

I knew I was in a minority position, but never thought it mattered all that much. It was a very friendly situation, and I didn't think that that would ever be an issue.

About nine years into this business relationship, the son took a vacation. And I thought that after the vacation we were going to talk about whether he wanted to get more involved in the business, as far as taking over. It had been his dad's business; I was in my mid-50s then and thought if he wanted to take it over, we'd work something out. He could run the business, and I could start to step aside—if the compensation was reasonable. We could work something out. We owned the building together, and we could keep that, so there was a lot of positive spin on it.

Well, he comes back from vacation, walks into my office that Monday morning, and advises me that I'm fired. Just like that. That was one of those jaw-dropping moments in life, when you say, "Excuse me? Are you kidding?"

He obviously believed he had a certain position to do that. He had apparently talked to the attorneys for months before, and kind of blindsided me on the whole thing. But it turned out I had the basis for a wrongful termination suit against him and forced him to settle the whole thing—the building, the business, the wrongful termination—all at the same time.

I came out of it very well because he miscalculated a few things. His dad and I had certain verbal agreements that other people were privileged to know also—they weren't a secret. And because of those agreements I didn't fit the category as just an employee.

But that moment in time, "You're fired," after nine years of building a business, is not a fun thing.

 The lesson is that it made me more cautious about getting into business with other people and understanding that being a minority, even if it's a 49 percent share, it's still a minority, and it doesn't give you the right to hold the position the rest of your life. If somebody else is in control and has a majority interest, it puts you at risk.

Now if I'm not going to be a majority partner, then it's just an investment to me. I don't put myself at risk as a working partner. If I feel something is of value and I buy a certain percentage of it, then I just do that. I don't get involved in any other part of the business. I just do it on the investment part. Then everybody has to follow the rules and you're subject to the normal accounting processes, and you're able to view people's books and make sure they're not doing anything they're not supposed to be doing. At least you're not at risk of having somebody tell you you've worked hard, but you're being fired.

About John Cappelletti

A defensive linebacker as a freshman and sophomore at Penn State, John Cappelletti was moved to running back in his junior year, 1972, and gained 1,117 yards. As a senior, he rushed for 1,522 yards, was a consensus All-American, and won the Heisman Trophy as the nation's outstanding college player. The six-foot-one, 219-pound Cappelletti joined the Los Angeles Rams in 1974 and was with them for five seasons. He missed 1979 with a knee injury and then spent three seasons with the San Diego Chargers before retiring. In his eight professional seasons, Cappelletti rushed 824 times for 2,751 yards, a 3.3 average, and 24 touchdowns. He caught 135 passes for 1,233 yards and four touchdowns.

At Penn State, Cappelletti put together three straight 200-yard rushing games in the final month of the season his senior year, including a high of 220 against North Carolina State. In 1973, Cappelletti received the Maxwell Trophy, which is presented annually to the outstanding player in collegiate football. Cappelletti was also selected as Player of the Year by ABC-TV, United Press International, the Philadelphia Sports Writers Association, the Walter Camp Foundation, and the Washington Touchdown Club. He also played in the Hula and Senior Bowl games. With a college career yardage total of 2,639, Cappelletti still holds a number of Penn State ground-gaining records.

The 1973 Heisman Trophy winner, John Cappelletti helped the Nittany Lions to a perfect 12-0 season and No.5 national ranking in both of the major polls. A consensus All-American, Cappelletti rushed for 1,522 yards and 17 touchdowns in 1973. Cappelletti majored in law enforcement and corrections.

Cappelletti's acceptance speech at the 1973 Heisman Dinner was considered the most moving ever given at these ceremonies, as he honored his younger brother Joey, who would later die of leukemia. A book and movie were later made about the experience (*Something for Joey*).

Professional Career

A first-round draft choice of the National Football League Los Angeles Rams, Cappelletti played eight seasons in the professional ranks, with Los Angeles and the San Diego Chargers.

Cappelletti was introduced into the National Football Foundation College Football Hall of Fame in 1993.

He resides in Laguna Niguel, California, and owns a classic car dealership in San Juan Capistrano.

Part Four
Personalities

Personalities are known more for who they are than the companies they've run—which in many cases may be their own. In fact, some personalities are businesses all by themselves.

They may not fit into a traditional category, but their thoughts and experiences can be valuable in the field of business. There are recognizable people here, like Dave Ramsey, who is an accomplished businessman but full of worldly advice from things that have gone wrong. Suze Orman, who is a corporation of financial advising unto herself (and frankly could easily fit into the Legends and Gurus section). Jim Cramer could appear in practically any category, first as a legend of sorts on Wall Street and the chief executive of TheStreet.com. But come on, how could I leave him out of a "Personalities" section? And there are brilliant and funny individuals like Ben Stein, who is as well educated as any comic actor anywhere, and who gives serious advice from the perspective of the schooled economist that he is.

There are columnists here, and people who tend to appear on talk shows to discuss everything under the sun. And though the folks here may not have run huge organizations or corporations, they've established a successful niche in a world full of competition trying to crowd them out. You've got to have some refined business savvy to do that.

23
SUZE ORMAN

Host of CNBC's *The Suze Orman Show*

Named by *Forbes* as one of the Most Influential Women in Media

Author of six consecutive *New York Times* best sellers

When you think about financial advice from somebody on television, on radio, or in print, one of the first names that comes to mind—if not *the* first—is Suze Orman.

You can see her on her own show on CNBC, on PBS raising money and giving motivational speeches, or visiting Oprah to offer financial guidance and give away free copies of her latest book on controlling your financial life.

But you may be one of those people who don't get Suze's popularity. You may not understand the allure of a TV show where she asks people whether they can afford a new car or a trip to the beach this summer.

It may not make sense to you why she:

- Has written six straight best sellers on managing your financial life.
- Is considered the biggest fund raiser on PBS.

- Is a frequent guest on *Oprah*.
- Has won two daytime Emmy Awards.
- Has won six Gracie Allen Awards.
- Was named by *Forbes* as one of the Most Influential Women in Media.
- Was picked by *Time* as one of the World's Most Influential People.

Let me explain her appeal. I learned it after getting to know her at CNBC. As an anchor on a daily basis I interviewed, on the one hand, money managers who would tout their latest approach to picking the right stocks. They would back-test their investment theories, prove their approaches were successful with charts and numbers that added or divided this into that, and generally impressed you with the most sophisticated discussion of financial investing you can imagine. On the other hand, there was Suze.

Suze Orman's appeal is simple: *She's not Wall Street!*

Suze doesn't look at Wall Street as the *answer*; she sees it as the *problem*.

Suze doesn't believe you should put your happiness in the hands of people you shouldn't trust. And it's not like she doesn't know the folks on Wall Street, because she used to be a stockbroker and financial adviser herself. She knows all about it because she's seen it up close, and she's here to tell you: *Look out!*

In fact, for many years, as the stock market ascended what became a bubble waiting to be burst, she was practically a lone voice telling you that stockbrokers and money managers do not have your best interests at heart. Says Suze,

Those people don't even know what to do with their own money. They might be good salespeople, but they don't know how to invest. They're nothing more than puppets for the brokerages.

A strange perspective, you might think, for a former stockbroker. But it was precisely that experience that stoked her fire for the little guy.

"It was 1983," she recalls. "I had worked for Merrill Lynch for three years. I had sold millions and millions of dollars of Baldwin United's annuity, and I thought it was the greatest thing I'd ever seen."

But then the financial newspapers started talking about the financial trouble Baldwin United was having. Suze recalls the stock falling from $62 to $2. As the stock was falling, she would go into her sales manager's office expressing her concerns and he would say, "Oh, Suze, please, we have a buy rating on the stock."

It turned out Baldwin United was, indeed, in trouble. It went belly-up. And all her clients were about to lose their money. She says:

> That pissed me off because they lied to me! So I made sure that as many clients as would do it became part of class action lawsuit in the state of California against all the brokerage firms. The good news is the suit was won and eventually all the people got their money back.

Suze relishes that kind of story. She likes to fight for the regular person. Her advice on investing is not about impressing you with charts and graphs and complex concepts that have been back-tested and are waiting for you to jump on.

Her advice is direct and simple. "People first, then money, then things," she says. And while she knows the world is full of Wall Street types who will try to get your money, she wants you to take control of your own investing future.

She made unofficial history on the *Oprah Winfrey Show* in 2009 by allowing people to download her book, *Women and Money*, free from Oprah's web site for 33 hours. More than one and a half million copies were downloaded.

Suze Orman's Best Mistake, in Her Own Words

My biggest mistake was also my best mistake. I was working at Prudential Bache. And there was a woman who was a financial consultant. She wasn't making it.

The manager at the time came to me—I was a vice president of investments. He said, "Suze, can you just take her on as your assistant? Maybe she could do something for you so we don't have to let her go, and we'll work out a deal." And I said okay, because I was doing a serious amount of business and I *did* need help.

 So I took her on even though I didn't like her. I never liked her. But I didn't listen to my gut. I was being a woman helping out another woman.

Then I decided to leave Prudential Bache and go on my own because it was ridiculous that I was giving them 60 percent of all my commissions when I was bringing in all the clients. I was the one doing everything; it was just nuts.

So I found the space, I had it decorated, and I was about to leave Prudential, but I didn't have the nerve to tell this person that I didn't like her, I didn't want her to come with me, and I didn't trust her. I didn't have the courage to tell her, so I brought her over.

We opened my firm on May 2, 1987. On June 22, I walked into my office, and this person had come into my office at one A.M. and ripped off every single file that I had. She directed the commissions to her. We had a lot of clients, and the way it was set up was that I would see the clients and tell them what to do, and they would then go into her office and she would make the investments with them and sign the contracts under her name. When the commission checks came in, she would deposit them into the office account (they were made out to her since she signed the contract), and I would get 80 percent of those commissions and she would get 20 percent—that's the deal we struck.

 The night after she came in and stole all the records of the clients, she also called the firm that was paying us the commissions and she instructed them to send those commissions checks to her at her home address. And there was nothing I could do about it since her name was on the contracts. She did everything she could to steal the business right out from under me.

That's when I learned that I should never talk myself into trusting anyone—that I should trust myself more than I trust others.

I knew in my gut that she was trouble, and I just did not listen to my gut. I did not trust myself enough to just follow what I felt. I kept talking myself into trusting her when I knew from the start I should not.

Because I took the chicken way out, I ended up screwing myself. And that was the biggest mistake I ever made that led to the best lesson that I have stuck with to this day. Now if somebody enters my life and I sense they're not good, they're out of there in two seconds.

 I trust myself more than I trust others.

About Suze Orman

Suze Orman has been called "a force in the world of personal finance" and "a one-woman financial advice powerhouse" by *USA Today*. A two-time Emmy Award-winning television host, *New York Times* mega best-selling author, magazine and online columnist, writer/producer, and one of the top motivational speakers in the world today, Orman is undeniably America's most recognized expert on personal finance.

Orman is a contributing editor to *O: The Oprah Magazine* and the *Costco Connection* magazine, and for the past eight years has hosted the award-winning *Suze Orman Show*, which airs every Saturday night on CNBC. Over her television career Suze has accomplished what no other television personality ever has before. Not only is she the single most successful fund-raiser in the history of public television, but she has also garnered an unprecedented six Gracie Allen Awards, more than anyone in the 34-year history of this prestigious award. The Gracies recognize the nation's best radio, television, and cable programming for, by, and about women.

In October 2008 Orman was the recipient of the National Equality Award from the Human Rights Campaign. In 2008 and 2009 *Time* magazine named Orman as one of the *Time* 100, the World's Most Influential People. In April 2008 Orman was presented with the Amelia Earhart Award for her message of financial empowerment for women, and *Saturday Night Live* spoofed Suze three times during 2008.

Orman, who grew up on the South Side of Chicago, earned a bachelor's degree in social work at the University of Illinois, and in 2009 received an honorary doctorate degree. At the age of 30, Suze was still a waitress making $400 a month.

Chapter 24
JIM CRAMER

Host of CNBC's *Mad Money with Jim Cramer*

Former successful hedge fund manager

Co-founded TheStreet.com

I s it an act? That's what I asked him, back before Jim Cramer joined CNBC as a host.

He had already become a well-known hedge fund manager and co-founder of TheStreet.com. He was a regular guest on *Squawk Box* as a co-host. But it was before his numerous books on investing in the stock market.

Before commercials appeared with takeoffs on his character on CNBC's show *Mad Money*.

Before CBS's *60 Minutes* did a profile on him.

Before his "They know nothing!" tirade against Ben Bernanke and company.

Before he went on the *Today* show in 2008 during the financial crisis and warned investors that they should take money out of the market if they needed it within the next five years.

Before he became a target—rightly or wrongly—of everyone from the Obama administration to Jon Stewart.

"I learned a long time ago," he told me, "that you have to make it interesting."

And he sure does that.

On his CNBC show *Mad Money*, while he's ranting and hyperventilating about stocks that you should buy or sell with haste, he looks like someone you'd avoid at the bus station. But here's the deal with Jim Cramer. Even off camera he's high energy, but he's one of the smartest people you'll ever meet.

And it's not like his path to Wall Street was a gilded path. This is a guy who worked as a print journalist. In fact, that's where he learned "to make it interesting." At one point in his life he spent nine months living out of his car. And while he searched for what he wanted to do with his life, he got a law degree from Harvard Law School.

Just because he punches bells and whistles for ratings on *Mad Money*, don't let that fool you into thinking that's all there is to Jim, or that it's a joke. The screaming shtick on TV belies his thoughtfulness when it comes to investing. He was a successful hedge fund manager way before he became a TV star. And while some critics will question the profitability of his stock recommendations on the show, keep in mind that Jim made serious money in *real life*. He knows more than virtually all his critics because he's actually done it. And he did it by being flexible in buying and selling, sometimes moving in and out of positions based on stock movements that ranged in the teenies (sixteenths of a point—remember when stocks traded that way?).

The biggest value that I've always seen in Jim's on-air work is that he can teach people how to think about stocks and the underlying companies as investments. Forget about whether his stock recommendations pay off—that's not how he made his millions.

He's trying to teach viewers how to evaluate companies and the stocks that provide investment opportunities. If you watch it with that approach in mind, you'll be better off than trying to day trade or position trade his recommendations.

And about his tirade about Bernanke. ("He has no idea how bad it is out there!") In retrospect, wasn't he right?

Jim doesn't actively manage money anymore, but from 1988 to 1997, he beat the S&P 500 every year. That includes the recession year of 1990, when his fund gained 12 percent even as the market fell 7 percent. And in 1995, while the S&P returned a solid 34 percent, his fund rose a scorching 60 percent.

Then came 1998.

Jim Cramer's Best Mistake, in His Own Words

[In 1998, the S&P rose 27 percent while Jim Cramer's fund returned a dismal 2 percent. He had ridden a formula to success that involved buying stock in the best savings and loans in the country. He would buy S&Ls that were trading lower than their book value.]

 We got into these savings and loans that we thought would either get bought or grow big. It had worked for the better part of a decade.

[But in 1998, low interest rates made it hard for S&Ls to make money on deposits, and the government began opposing consolidation in the S&L industry.]

Everything that had been working stopped working. . . . Investors were calling for updates minute by minute. . . . We ended up losing in an earnings fashion *and* in a take-over fashion. Our portfolio was just bad.

 In the middle of 1998 I went to my partner, Jeff Berkowitz. We admitted to mak-ing a blunder and agreed that "We don't like what we're doing here."

Either the market was incredibly overvalued and we should give the money back, or we should accept the fact that our methodology was flawed. It's considered heresy to change styles. But we had to do it.

We had these soul-searching sessions nightly. We'd go over our stock positions one by one. We would black out the winners and talk about why the *losers* were bad picks. We had to go to our investors and tell them the methodology that we'd used for a long time wasn't working. It wasn't easy. Can we admit that we did something wrong, and have the investors stick with us? A lot of them didn't. We had $100 million taken out in one day. It was horrible. It was mind-numbing. The faxes piled up with sell orders and wiring instructions.

It was gut-wrenching for me because for the most part the people who left me had been with me since 1982. About a third of our investors pulled out. I was just crushed by it.

But the change worked. We started buying tech stocks. We tried to figure out what companies were going to beat earnings forecasts by the biggest amount, and took big positions. In 1999, the S&P gained 20 percent—we were up 62 percent! And in 2000, when the NASDAQ tanked 11 percent, we started shorting [betting against] tech stocks and gained 36 percent.

 We had made a colossal mistake, and a lot of people pulled out. But we took an honest look at what we were doing, and it saved the firm.

About Jim Cramer

Jim Cramer graduated magna cum laude from Harvard College, where he was president of the *Harvard Crimson*. He worked as a journalist at the *Tallahassee Democrat* and the *Los Angeles Herald Examiner*, covering everything from sports to homicide, before moving to New York to help start *American Lawyer* magazine. After a three-year stint, Mr. Cramer entered Harvard Law School and received his JD in 1984. Instead of practicing law, however, he joined Goldman Sachs, where he worked in sales and trading. In 1987 he left Goldman to start his own hedge fund. While he worked at his fund, Mr. Cramer helped start *Smart Money* for Dow Jones, and then in 1996 he co-founded TheStreet.com, of which he is chairman, and where he has served as a columnist and contributor ever since.

In 2000, Mr. Cramer retired from active money management to embrace media full-time, including radio and television. Currently, he is a markets commentator for CNBC and TheStreet.com. In addition to his daily writing for TheStreet.com's *RealMoney* and *Action Alerts PLUS*, as well as his participation in various video segments on TheStreet.com TV, he serves as host of CNBC's *Mad Money* television program.

Mr. Cramer is the author of *Confessions of a Street Addict, You Got Screwed, Jim Cramer's Real Money, Jim Cramer's Mad Money, Jim Cramer's Stay Mad for Life*, and recently published *Jim Cramer's Getting Back to Even*. He is a frequent contributor to *New York* magazine. He has been featured on *60 Minutes, Nightly News with Brian Williams, Meet the Press with Tim Russert, The Tonight Show with Jay Leno, Late Night with Conan O'Brien*, NBC's *Today with Matt Lauer and Meredith Vieira*, and MSNBC's *Morning Joe*.

Chapter 25

MARK CUBAN

Created Broadcast.com

Sold Broadcast.com to Yahoo!, becoming a billionaire

Owner of NBA's Dallas Mavericks

Let's face it, Mark Cuban is living the life most of us middle-aged guys wish we had. He created a dot-com company that sold for billions, and now owns a professional basketball team, the Dallas Mavericks, where he gets to watch NBA games courtside and scream at the refs when they get a call wrong. Does life get better than that?

Oh sure, he gets in a little trouble sometimes. Like when he goes a bit too far, finding himself on the floor, mixing it up with the opposing players and criticizing the refs to the media after the game. He might even get fined by the league a few hundred thousand dollars every now and then—for a total of more than $1.5 million! But does that bother a guy with plenty of dot.com scrill to pay the fine?

And he's willing to pay for his verbal liberties in other ways, too. Like when he riffed that the NBA's manager of officials "wouldn't be able to manage a

Dairy Queen." The problem with that wasn't with the league—it was with management at Dairy Queen. So he spent a day working at a DQ mixing Blizzards and serving up chocolate dipped cones. What a lot of people might not know is that to this guy from Pittsburgh, blue collar work is not new, it's second nature.

His father was an automobile upholsterer. And Mark spent time as a salesman, a bartender, a party promoter, and a disco dance instructor. (That may explain his appearance as a contestant on ABC's *Dancing with the Stars*.)

He didn't make any real money until he started a company in the 1980s, called MicroSolutions, a computer consulting business. He sold that company in 1990 and made his first million (two, actually). It wasn't until later he made his first *billion*.

Even now Mark comes across as a blue-collar guy. You can take the kid out of Pittsburgh, but you can never take the Burgh out of the kid. But he isn't your average guy from anywhere. He thinks creatively. He puts energy into what he does. And his big personality seems to bring it all together.

Consider how he helped finance his college education at Indiana University. With chain letters.

"They're definitely a Ponzi scheme," Mark told me. "But they helped me learn a whole lot about how markets work."

In the 1990s he started Broadcast.com because he wanted to see—and have the right to broadcast—Indiana University basketball games. He eventually sold the company to Yahoo! for almost $6 billion in stock. But if he hadn't thought ahead, he would have been road kill on the bombed-out highway that the dot-coms took.

How did Mark stay a billionaire? After he got all his Yahoo! stock, he bought put options just in case it went down. It did, about 90 percent worth. So he stayed a billionaire while the air went out of the dot-com bubble.

Mark has made a fortune, but he's not a software geek. He's a businessman, who almost *wasn't* a businessman.

Mark Cuban's Best Mistake, in His Own Words

In my junior year in college, my friends and I used to throw these parties, just as party promoters. We weren't 21 yet, but they'd let us into these bars and we'd take the cover charge, and we were making a lot of money.

So over that summer, I said to a friend, "You know what? We should just go for it."
And that's exactly what we did.

 My senior year we were able to take over a bar. My friend put in money and I
put in my student loan money and we opened up a bar called Motley's Pub, in
Dunkirk Square in Bloomington, Indiana.

It turned into the hottest bar on campus. It was going great. Then came February 12,
1979. I'll never forget it. We had a wet T-shirt contest, and the place was packed to the
rafters. I remember thinking, you know what, I better be really, really careful. Because I'm
sure we're going to get a lot of attention from the authorities, not only because we were
running a wet T-shirt contest, but because we were killing the business of all these other
local drinking establishments.

I made sure I did all the carding myself of the girls who were in the T-shirt contest.
I remember carding the very first girl who came in. I was thinking, okay, she looks a little
young but her ID is legit.

 So we had the wet T-shirt contest and it went off without a hitch. But the local
newspaper decided to take pictures. And this one picture showed the three
finalists—in full dress, by the way! It turns out that a probation officer saw
the article and recognized one of the three girls as being 16 years old and on
probation for prostitution. And they came down on me like a ton of bricks. That
basically ended my bar-owning career.

And I am thankful for every minute of every day that that happened. Rather than all
the amazing things that have happened to me since then, I might still be running that bar
in Bloomington, Indiana! It's the best mistake I ever made.

About Mark Cuban

When Mark Cuban purchased the Dallas Mavericks on January 14, 2000, the
face of the organization began to change immediately. Once again Mavericks
games had a party atmosphere as Reunion Arena rocked with the return of the
"Reunion Rowdies." Mavericks games became more than just ordinary NBA
games—they were a total entertainment experience.

Cuban was not only successful at instilling a sense of pride and passion
into Mavericks fans by presenting himself as the ultimate role model by

cheering from the same seats he had in years past, but he also became the first owner in team sports to encourage fan interaction through e-mail on his personal computer. It was through this personal touch that fans throughout the Metroplex, and around the world, began to notice Cuban's energetic personality and take notice of the Mavericks. He has personally responded to thousands of e-mails, and several suggestions from fans have led to innovative changes such as a new three-sided shot clock, which allows line of sight to the 24-second clock from anywhere in the arena.

Cuban's whatever-it-takes attitude and commitment to winning has everyone's attention. From his first introduction to the team to the end of his first season as owner, the players responded with a 31–19 record, including a 9–1 mark in April 2000. In addition to hiring special coaches for offense, defense, and shooting, Cuban has promised to do everything in his power to improve the team. This goal was achieved as the club finished the 2000–2001 season with a 53–29 record en route to their first playoff appearance in 11 years, where they became just the sixth team in NBA history to be down 0–2 and come back to win a five-game series versus Utah in round 1.

Before the start of the 2001–2002 season, American Airlines Center, the Mavs' new home, opened and Cuban co-founded HDNet, an all-high-definition television network on DIRECTV Channel 199, which launched in September 2001. As with his other ventures, Cuban is revolutionizing the television industry with HDNet.

During the Mavs 2001-02 campaign, the team continued their winning ways by finishing the season with a franchise-best record of 57-25 and an NBA-best road record of 27-14, advancing to the postseason for the second-consecutive year.

Prior to his purchase of the Mavericks, Cuban co-founded Broadcast.com, the leading provider of multimedia and streaming on the Internet, in 1995, selling it to Yahoo! in July of 1999. Before Broadcast.com, Cuban co-founded MicroSolutions, a leading National Systems Integrator, in 1983, and later sold it to CompuServe.

Today, in addition to his ownership of the Mavericks, Cuban is an active investor in leading and cutting-edge technologies and continues to be a sought-after speaker.

Chapter 26
BEN STEIN

Speechwriter for two U.S. presidents

Author, actor, lawyer, economist, columnist

He was also Ferris Bueller's what? Anyone . . .

When I interviewed him for this book, I just had to ask Ben Stein something that had been on my mind. Several years ago I was anchoring a cable business show and he was one of the guests. He was joining us from a studio in Los Angeles and at one point I asked him a question, but he didn't respond. So I went with the obvious: "Bueller . . . Bueller . . ."

Crickets. And when he did finally say something, he didn't reference it. So I figured I must have ticked him off by reducing this accomplished author, lawyer, columnist, and economist to his iconic role as the boring teacher in *Ferris Bueller's Day Off*.

"No, not at all," he told me. "I didn't hear you. If I had I would have said something. I love being teased about Ferris Bueller and I will never get tired of it."

That surprised me a little bit because it's not the most creative thing a person could throw his way. "No," he says. "I go through the airport and people say 'Bueller . . . Bueller . . .' all day long to me and I never get tired of it. I like the attention. I don't want to be anonymous; I want the attention."

That's one of the engaging things about Ben Stein—his sense of humor. In fact, when he says something serious, sometimes it still sounds funny. When he rails against a politician as a guest on CNN or Fox News Channel, it often sounds so humorous that you can't always tell at first whether it's tongue in cheek or earnest. That's part of what makes him such an interesting person to talk with.

After all, this is a highly educated man. The son of noted economist Herb Stein, Ben graduated from Columbia University with honors in economics, and graduated from Yale Law School as well. He has worked as an economist at the Department of Commerce, has been a trial lawyer at the Federal Trade Commission, and has taught economics or law at American University, Pepperdine, and the University of California at Santa Cruz.

He has written dozens of books, including seven novels, and once served as a speechwriter and lawyer for Richard Nixon. He has been a contributor to *Barron's* and a columnist for the *Wall Street Journal*, the *Los Angeles Herald Examiner*, the *New York Times*, *New York* magazine, and the *American Spectator*. He was the star of his own television game show on Comedy Central, *Win Ben Stein's Money*, and is a commentator for *CBS Sunday Morning* and Fox News.

I could go on and on with his accomplishments, but the point is this: John F. Kennedy once assembled Nobel laureates at the White House dining room. He is famously quoted as saying, "I think this is the most extraordinary collection of talent, of human knowledge, that has ever been gathered together at the White House, with the possible exception of when Thomas Jefferson dined alone."

Maybe Ben Stein isn't Thomas Jefferson, but he is probably a better actor and a whole lot funnier than the group that JFK dined with. Yet he is charmingly realistic in knowing what people will remember him for. He says:

> I expect that on my gravestone it will just say, "Ben Stein" and it will give my dates and then it'll say "Bueller . . . Bueller . . ."

And that's fine with me.

In recent years his conservative political leanings have not always gone over well in the mainstream media. Take his column in the *New York Times*

Business Section. They dropped it after objecting to Ben's participation in TV commercials.

"That was a total political smear," he says. "For them to say I can't make TV commercials, after I had been making TV commercials for twenty years when they hired me, was just unbelievable. And they would ask me for souvenirs from the TV commercials! So for them to say, 'Oh, we didn't know you were going to do TV commercials!' My editor has a collection of souvenirs from those commercials!"

As a loyal reader of his former Sunday column, I still miss reading it. And when I brought it up to Ben it was clear he remained irked by the gray lady. I felt a little bad talking about it, and I'm a little ashamed to say that when he spoke of it with considerable annoyance—it was still kind of funny.

Bueller?

Ben Stein's Best Mistake, in His Own Words

In 1978, my wife and I bought a beautiful house at Sixth and Hallam in Aspen, Colorado. It was a very beautiful house. The market was terribly weak and we got an incredibly good buy on it. I think we paid something like $270,000 for a beautiful house in Aspen.

We kept it for a while; we had nothing but aggravation. The contractor that was renovating it ripped us off mercilessly—MERCILESSLY! The neighbors one time when we were out of town tried to seize by adverse possession a couple hundred square feet of our property. We rented it out during the ski season and various people mistreated it. . . .

 We just thought, "You know, this is more aggravation than it's worth, and besides, Aspen is *done* for, nothing much seems to be happening here, it's a has-been town." So we sold it for maybe a hundred thousand more than we paid for it. Within 10 years it was worth *10 times* what we had paid for it.

The reason that turns out to be a colossal business mistake, way beyond what it might seem to be, is that in the meantime I've bought many, many, many other pieces of real estate, and I never sell them. And that's turned out to be a big mistake, too! Because now that real estate is a drug [*sic*] on the market, it's not the world's greatest idea to be holding anywhere near as much real estate as I do. I have a startling number of homes, and quite a bit of commercial property.

And the lesson I learned in Aspen of never selling turned out to *not* be the right lesson! My lessons almost always have to do with taking the *wrong* lesson from a situation.

Long ago my incredibly smart father [Herb Stein, former chairman of the Council of Economic Advisers under President Nixon and President Ford] told me something that I should have borne in mind, which was, "Every time there's inflation, including in real estate, there is one inevitable corollary to the rule of inflation, which is that all inflations end." I keep forgetting that all inflations end! But of course, they always start up again, so I'm hoping I live long enough to see it start up again.

There is positive out of this Aspen thing, though, because if I net out all the losses I've had in real estate and then subtract them from all the gain I've had in real estate, the gains still greatly outnumber losses.

 The lesson that I learned in Aspen, which is I sold too early, has stood me in good stead, because even though I've lost money in things I've bought in the past few years, if you take the things I've bought in the last twenty years, the gains have been quite good.

About Ben Stein

Benjamin J. Stein was born November 25, 1944, in Washington, D.C., the son of the economist and writer Herbert Stein; he grew up in Silver Spring, Maryland, and attended Montgomery Blair High School. He graduated from Columbia University in 1966 with honors in economics. He graduated from Yale Law School in 1970 as valedictorian of his class by election of his classmates. He also studied in the graduate school of economics at Yale. He has worked as an economist at The Department of Commerce, a poverty lawyer in New Haven and Washington, D.C., a trial lawyer in the field of trade regulation at the Federal Trade Commission in Washington, D.C., a university adjunct at American University in Washington, D.C., at the University of California at Santa Cruz (UCSC), and at Pepperdine University in Malibu, California. At American University he taught about the political and social content of mass culture. He taught the same subject at the UCSC, as well as about political and civil rights under the Constitution. At Pepperdine, he has taught about libel law and about securities law and ethical issues since 1986.

In 1973 and 1974, he was a speechwriter and lawyer for Richard Nixon at the White House and then for Gerald Ford. (He did *not* write the line "I am not a crook.") He has been a columnist and editorial writer for the *Wall Street Journal*, a syndicated columnist for the *Los Angeles Herald Examiner* (R.I.P.) and King Features Syndicate, and a frequent contributor to *Barron's*, where his articles about the ethics of management buyouts and issues of fraud in the Milken Drexel junk bond scheme drew major national attention. He has been a regular columnist for *Los Angeles* magazine, *New York* magazine, E! Online, and most of all, has written a lengthy diary for 20 years for the *American Spectator*. He currently writes a column for the *New York Times* Sunday Business Section and has for many years, a column about personal finance for Yahoo!, is a commentator for *CBS Sunday Morning*, and for Fox News.

He has written, co-written, and published 30 books, including seven novels, largely about life in Los Angeles, and 21 nonfiction books, about finance and about ethical and social issues in finance, and also about the political and social content of mass culture. He has done pioneering work in uncovering the concealed messages of TV and in explaining how TV and movies get made. His titles include *A License to Steal, Michael Milken and the Conspiracy to Bilk the Nation, The View from Sunset Boulevard, Hollywood Days, Hollywood Nights, DREEMZ, Financial Passages*, and *Ludes*. His most recent books are the best-selling humor self-help series, *How to Ruin Your Life*. He has also been a longtime screen-writer, writing, among many other scripts (most of which were unmade), the first draft of *The Boost*, a movie based on *Ludes*, and the outlines of the lengthy miniseries *Amerika* and the acclaimed *Murder in Mississippi*. He was one of the creators of the well-regarded comedy *Fernwood Tonight*.

He is also an extremely well-known actor in movies, TV, and commercials. His part of the boring teacher in *Ferris Bueller's Day Off* was recently ranked as one of the 50 most famous scenes in American film. From 1997 to 2002, he was the host of the Comedy Central quiz show, *Win Ben Stein's Money*. The show won seven Emmys. He was a judge on CBS's *Star Search*, and on VH-1's *America's Most Smartest Model*.

He lives with his wife, Alexandra Denman (a former lawyer), six cats, and three large dogs in Beverly Hills. He is active in pro-animal and pro-life charitable events.

Chapter 27

ARIANNA HUFFINGTON

Founder, HuffingtonPost.com

On list of *Forbes*'s "Most Influential Women in Media"

Author, columnist, candidate for governor of California

Those of us who are baby boomers remember a time when political debate was pure. Oh, that's not to say that politics wasn't a dirty game—it always has been. But before radio show hosts feigned political outrage for the sake of stirring up antigovernment sentiment, or Capitol Hill operatives launched ad campaigns designed to turn out the base on election day, political debate was engaged in by highly educated, accomplished, erudite, and idealistically thoughtful participants. (Sure, it's idealistic. But humor me here, it's a good story.) It was an intellectual remnant of the 1960s revolution that lasted into the 1970s. And for one day, an undergraduate named Arianna Huffington found herself in the middle of it. She learned a lesson from it that stays with her even now.

"In my Cambridge years, as an undergraduate," she says, "I was in the debating society, and I was chosen to make the opening speech on J. K. Galbraith's side against Bill Buckley."

John Kenneth Galbraith was literally a friend of the Kennedys. He was a noted liberal economist who believed in the power of the government to right many of the ills of society and the inequities of the free market. He served under Democratic presidents and published popular books on economics with intellectually progressive arguments that he espoused as a professor at Harvard. His liberal credentials were as tall as he was, which was roughly three inches shy of seven feet.

William F. Buckley, in contrast, was a giant among conservatives. His wit and intelligence made him an almost untouchable opponent in the arena of political discourse on his television show, *Firing Line*. His libertarian advocacy helped form the foundation of movements within the Republican Party that led to the rise of leaders like Ronald Reagan himself.

"It was one of those debates taped for Buckley's show," Arianna recalls. "I spoke, then Galbraith spoke, then Buckley spoke, and he was dripping smoothness and self-assurance, and proceeded to tear Galbraith into elegant little pieces.

"So I was sitting next to Galbraith, and at one point he prodded me to interrupt Buckley and explain in some academic way that the conditions he was describing applied only to the stock exchange and that all other markets were imperfect. Instinctively I knew it wasn't right because I knew that wasn't the nature of the debate, but Cambridge Union rules are that if someone stands, the speaker has to give way and allow them to interrupt you. So Buckley gave way, I interrupted him, and I made my point.

"Then Buckley turned to me and said, 'Madam, I do not know what market you patronize.' It brought the house down. To this day I'm not sure what he meant, but I was completely humbled. And I thought my days as a Cambridge debater were over.

"The lessons that it taught me were: One, don't do anything against your better judgment, even if it's a distinguished professor and you're a mere under-graduate. And two, it's never over unless *you* think it's over. Don't lose out on the chance for redemption, a shot at coming back and trying again."

Reinventing herself is something Arianna is rather well known for. As would be expected by anyone who spoke on the side of John Kenneth Galbraith, she was on the liberal side of most arguments in the 1970s. But later on, further into the 1980s and 1990s, she became a well-known supporter of Republican causes (she was married for a time to conservative politician Michael Huffington). She was an active and vocal advocate for Newt Gingrich's revolution and Bob Dole's candidacy for president in 1996. But in the late 1990s her positions began to change back to her progressive roots. Now she's a Democrat again who believes in the potential positive power of the government.

Through it all, she tells me her overriding goal has been "to create a more fair and just society, and to care for those in need." She just stopped believing that the conservative movement could accomplish that. And she's happy to debate the point, because she believes in it.

Galbraith and Buckley would have been proud.

Arianna Huffington's Best Mistake, in Her Own Words

One of the big failures—mistakes—in my own life was with my second book. It came after a successful first book.

My first book was on the changing world of women (*The Female Woman*). For my second book (*After Reason*) I really wanted to write about the role of political leadership. It was a book that nobody else wanted me to write, but I was really drawn to do it. You can imagine my surprise when it was rejected by publisher after publisher. Thirty-six publishers turned it down before it was finally published.

It was the kind of rejection that brought up all kinds of self-doubt, including fear that I not only was on the wrong career path, but was going to go broke in the process. And I had thoughts like, was the success of the first book a fluke? And I would ask myself in the middle of many a sleepless night, was I even meant to *be* a writer?

I had used the royalties from my first book to subsidize writing the second; then at some point that money was running out. My choice was that I would have to try to find a real job (and give up on the book), or continue to hope that I could make writing work.

I was living in London at the time, and I remember walking down James Street. And I passed by Barclay's bank, and something just made me walk into the bank and ask for an overdraft [loan].

I remember meeting this banker there, Ian Bell. It was like in a fairy tale, where you have all these helpful people who suddenly appear, and he was that type of person. And he gave me an overdraft (loan)—I'm sure he still doesn't know why—but every Christmas I still send him a Christmas card.

The overdraft allowed me to keep myself going while I kept trying to find another publisher. I was writing more letters, and meeting with more publishers in England trying to sell the book. I didn't have an agent; I didn't have anybody to represent me. Without an overdraft, I would really have had to take some kind of other job and give up on the book. Instead, it made it possible for me to continue to try to get the book published. And I did.

The book did not do well, but it became like a seed that was planted in my twenties, and finally sprouted in my forties when I became seriously engaged in political life and began writing about it. A lot of what I wrote then became the foundation of my thinking later.

Q.   That's interesting, considering you're noted for having shifted your political positions.

Yes, but at the heart of my political positions, both when I was a Republican and when I left the Republican Party, was the need to create a more fair and just society, and to care for those in need. When I was a Republican I thought we could best do this through private-sector solutions. Actually the main reason I left the Republican Party was because I realized that it wasn't happening fast enough. We really needed the raw power of government appropriations.

[Thirty-some years later, her experience informs her politics and her business ventures, including her web site, HuffingtonPost.com.]

I see it as learning from your failures. It goes beyond mistakes, because so often it is that fear of failing that makes us afraid to take risks that may turn out to be the best thing we did.

 Jumping in and doing what you love happens in the end only if you overcome the fear of failing.

About Arianna Huffington

Arianna Huffington is the co-founder and editor-in-chief of the Huffington Post, a nationally syndicated columnist, and author of 12 books. She is also co-host of *Left, Right & Center*, public radio's popular political roundtable program, and is a frequent guest on television shows such as *Charlie Rose*, *Real Time with Bill Maher*, *Larry King Live*, *Countdown with Keith Olbermann*, and the *Rachel Maddow Show*. In May 2005, she launched the Huffington

Post, a news and blog site that has quickly become one of the most widely read, linked to, and frequently cited media brands on the Internet. In 2006, she was named to the *Time* 100, *Time* magazine's list of the world's 100 most influential people. In 2008, she was named Media Person of the Year by I Want Media, and wrote the Introduction to *The Huffington Post Complete Guide to Blogging*. Originally from Greece, she moved to England when she was 16 and graduated from Cambridge University with an MA in economics. At 21, she became president of the famed debating society, the Cambridge Union.

Chapter 28
HERB GREENBERG

Columnist at *Fortune*, the *Wall Street Journal*, MarketWatch, TheStreet.com

Commentator on CNBC's *Mad Money*, panelist on Fox News Channel's *TheStreet.com*

Co-founder of GreenbergMeritz Research & Analytics

'll never write a book," Herb Greenberg tells me. In fact, he has told me that maybe 50 times. "Everybody writes a book. They put their heart and soul into it and then it sells five thousand copies. It's not worth the trouble."

As a first-time author, I'm sure hoping he's wrong. But even more than that, I hope he changes his mind and writes a book, because a lot of people could make—or save—some serious money because of what he knows.

If you have watched any business television over the past 15 years, or read any business publications for about 30 years, chances are that you've seen Herb's face or read his words somewhere. I met him in the late 1990s when he was a frequent guest on CNBC. (I'm happy to still call him a friend. My wife and I—before our kids—once enjoyed a Christmas-day dinner at his house with his family. How many people can say they had Christmas dinner at the *Greenbergs'*?)

During a period of time in which virtually everybody was ecstatic over this newfangled thing called the Internet, a never-ending stream of stock analysts would come on to tout the latest dot-com idea where you could get rich by taking an investment plunge with this or that new company. Herb refused to join the party. He never drank from the spiked punch bowl.

In fact, he was often deployed by bookers and producers as the foil to the gleeful fraternity of television stock pickers who liked to needle Herb's anti-bubble sentiment—even as they stayed away from the details of his arguments. "Ahhh, Herb, that's crazy!" they would sometimes laugh. And I know this because I anchored some of the segments and saw the reaction to him trying to bring honest-to-goodness dissection of balance sheets to the conversation. Remember, this was a time when the so-called new paradigm meant that quaint things like revenue and profit were a relic of the bricks-and-mortar past.

But Herb would never take it personally, laughing right back at them, because he knew from his reporting and looking at public documents issued by struggling companies for the previous 20 years that when he saw something that didn't add up, it was a red flag that wouldn't go away just by wishing it so.

He threw up red flags on well-known companies like Tyco, E*Trade, and MBIA, Inc., and lesser-known companies like Learnout and Hauspie, Media Vision and AremiSoft. (Herb: "One of the biggest frauds you've never heard of.")

And what does he look for? It's more of an art than a science.

"As a journalist, remember—my info always started with tips or ideas from Wall Street, employees of companies, or others," he says, adding:

There are so many different scenarios that make for the perfect story or situation. Aggressive accounting is always a red flag; obsession with a stock price; bonuses based on easy-to-meet metrics that can be maneuvered; products that are sold into saturated markets. No one size fits all.

Herb recalls, "Media Vision, whose CEO and CFO would end up going to jail, was busted wide open when a former employee came to my office and showed me a second set of books, and that's *after* I had been writing about receivables rising faster than sales and other aggressive warning signs."

He has always tried to stay a step ahead of companies as they paint a happy face on balance sheets or income statements that are full of financial frowns. And being a step ahead of others has been a trait of his TV career as well.

Herb was on Jim Cramer's *Mad Money* on CNBC for a year, the San Diego–based component of the "East vs. West" segment, "before anybody watched the show," he says.

"I was on *Fast Money* for a year before anybody watched it. I'm the guy who comes into the show when no one watches it. I was on *TheStreet.com* show on Fox before it became *Bulls and Bears*—before it became a one-million-viewer show.

"I do everything for a year, I leave, and then they get big," he says, reflecting his typical modesty.

Herb's earnest efforts as a business journalist were rewarded rather immo-destly at one point with some stock options at the TheStreet.com, where he was hired as a columnist.

But as a journalist, he was reluctant to sell the company's stock.

"When the stock was at a very high level, if I had sold the stock, I would have had to file public documents and it would have shown publicly how much stock I had," he says. "And it would have shown how much I was selling and how much I was making. For a journalist that would have been perceived as a considerable amount of money and probably would have raised a few eyebrows and garnered a line somewhere in somebody's column. You always risk that in journalism if you're perceived to be paid highly."

But if he could go back and do it over again, he probably would have pulled the trigger on selling the stock sooner. By waiting, he estimates he sold his stock at a level that was 25 to 30 percent of what he would have received had he sold earlier, which meant he left a lot of money on the table.

"I learned I don't owe anybody anything in not selling it."

It may have been a costly mistake, but not his best one. That came at the beginning of his career, before he became a writer for the *San Francisco Chronicle*, the *Chicago Tribune*, the *Wall Street Journal*, TheStreet.com, Market-Watch, and *Fortune* magazine. What he did back then helped launch a business journalism career that informs his work even now as the co-founder of the independent investment research firm GreenbergMeritz Research & Analytics.

You can be sure he's finding some red flags, and you won't read about them in a book.

"I'll never write a book."

Yes, Herb, I know, I know. But you should.

Herb Greenberg's Best Mistake, in His Own Words

In 1975 I took a year off from my first year as a reporter at a small daily newspaper in Florida to work at a trade publication in Nashville. But a year later I wanted to go back to daily newspapers and to go work for a Knight Ridder property.

Having gone to school on a scholarship from the *Miami Herald*, I went to Knight Ridder and asked for help. They lined me up with several interviews, including one to work on the city desk of the *Detroit Free Press*. You have to understand, in those days it was like saying you had an interview at the *New York Times*. Maybe not quite the same level, but the *DFP* had a reputation as one of the best newspapers in the country. It had some of the best editors and staffs in the country, right up there with the *Philadelphia Enquirer* and the *Miami Herald*.

I flew up for an interview and, well, I blew it. I was in the wrong place at the wrong time. They were just the wrong situation for me. Had I gone there and interviewed as a business reporter, I may have had a much better chance, but I think I was still green.

I took a series of tests that I later learned I had done extremely poorly on.

 When the managing editor asked me what my good traits were, I said, "Dependable."

"My dog is dependable," he shot back at me.

The minute I said "dependable" I knew I was dead. When he said, in effect, "So is my dog," I knew this job opportunity was going nowhere.

So then he had me sit out in the newsroom for a few hours and I was feeling like an absolute fool. You're not prepared for this, to just sit in the middle of a newsroom at a desk and wait, so that you could maybe see someone else. So I finally met with the executive editor—and by that point my ego was probably beaten up a little bit, and I felt like I was in the wrong place. Again, a terrible interview.

I flew back to Nashville and didn't hear anything for a week or two. So I called the city editor and I will never forget his words: "Frankly, we think we can find somebody better."

Talk about a motivator! I vowed then that I would get revenge, and the best revenge is making them wish they had hired me.

Not long after that I interviewed at the *St. Paul Pioneer Press*, another Knight Ridder paper. This time I applied for a slot on the business desk. Remember—in those days, business news was still the behind-the-sports-pages backwaters of journalism. I also had a big bushy head of hair—not quite the right look for a business reporter in Minnesota.

Well, I went up and interviewed and didn't hear back. So I pestered the business editor (who has since become a dear friend). And pestered him. And pestered him—until he hired me!

St. Paul was a mini-Chicago for business news. It was the perfect place to start, as business news started to come into its own. I was tossed in and covered retail (Dayton Hudson, now Target); food companies like Pillsbury and General Mills; 3M, which was *my* beat; and two airlines (Northwest and North Central, then a regional carrier).

You couldn't pay for that kind of experience. *Plus* I met my future wife in St. Paul.

 And then it happened: I started seeing my stories, which would regularly run on the Knight-Ridder newswire, appear in the *Detroit Free Press* and in newspapers around the country. It felt like that was the sweetest revenge.

I was then recruited away to *Crain's Chicago Business* and was later hired on the business desk of the *Chicago Tribune*. Later I became the *Trib*'s New York financial correspondent on my way to a 10-year stint as the lead business columnist at the *San Francisco Chronicle*, a five-year freelance column at *Fortune* magazine, a contributor job at CNBC, plus columnist stints at TheStreet.com in its early days and, later, MarketWatch. Oh, and for several years I had a Saturday column in the *Wall Street Journal*, before leaving to start my own investment research firm.

 You might say that the best thing that ever happened to me was screwing up those interviews and *not* getting hired in Detroit.

The mistake was being ill-prepared for that type of interviewing process, going to a place that was probably a little more sophisticated than I was ready for. My interviewing style, the lack of confidence—that was all a mistake.

Q.   So if you had followed your gut, would your gut have said go, or would it have said not to go?

That's a good question, because if I had to do it all over again I wouldn't have gone. On the other hand, it's part of the process. You're going to make those mistakes, and if you don't make those mistakes, you're not going to learn and you're not going to grow. And you're not going to take chances. So you have to sometimes go through those stupid interviews, where you say stupid things, to get better.

Q.   How were you different in the St. Paul interview?

I learned a lot about confidence from that Detroit interview, and that if you don't go into an interview with confidence you're not going to get hired. You can't go in there and feel like a patsy. You can't feel like you're beneath them. You've got to go in there and try to wow them.

In those days I was just learning. I never would have perceived myself as an aggressive digger. Today, let's just say the best compliment I get is when people complain that I ask too many questions.

"Dependable." *Ugh.*

About Herb Greenberg

Herb Greenberg is a veteran business journalist, best known for red-flagging companies. Before co-creating GreenbergMeritz, he wrote the "Weekend Investor" column for the *Wall Street Journal* and was senior columnist for MarketWatch.com, where his market blog attracted a large national following. Herb also has written financial columns for *Fortune* magazine, TheStreet.com, and the *San Francisco Chronicle* and was the New York financial correspondent for the *Chicago Tribune*. He also spent a year in the late 1980s as an analyst for an arbitrage firm. According to one study by Harvard University, Herb is the only individual reporter whose stories preceded Securities and Exchange Commission (SEC) investigations into accounting issues more than once. Until starting GreenbergMeritz, he was also a regular contributor to CNBC-TV, appearing on numerous shows, including *Fast Money* and *Mad Money*. A native of Miami, Florida, he holds a BA degree in journalism from the University of Miami.

Chapter 29
ARTHUR LAFFER

One of *Time* magazine's "Greatest Minds of the 20th Century"

Member of President Reagan's Economic Policy Advisory Board

Popularized the Laffer curve and supply-side economics

A rthur Laffer tends to stir things up wherever he goes—and he does it with a smile. When I spoke with him, he had just gotten off the air with MSNBC, talking about—what else?—economics and politics.

When I saw him, he was grinning. "I don't think I gave them exactly what they wanted," he chuckled. "At one point they wanted me to bash Clinton, but I supported Clinton!"

Indeed he did, and that stirred up a lot of Republicans who always thought he was one of them. After all, didn't he help write Proposition 13, the late-1970s populist voter initiative in California that limited how high property taxes could rise in the Golden State?

Didn't he promote the so-called Laffer curve and supply-side economics, which held that reducing federal taxes spurs economic growth and increases federal revenues? Didn't President Ronald Reagan's belief in that theory give him a driving argument to drastically cut tax rates for most Americans and

189

American businesses in the early 1980s? Wasn't he literally a Reagan economic adviser, for goodness' sake?

Yep. That's the guy. Then how could he stand up for Clinton? "For one thing," he says, "he cut a lot of government spending as a share of GDP and brought us into surplus. And he cut capital gains taxes."

Of course, Laffer's support of Clinton may have had something to do with Clinton's opponent, George H.W. Bush. Let's just say Bush 41 was not a Laffer fan. He once called supply-side theories "voodoo economics." Do I have to tell you who Laffer voted for in 1992? He says he voted for Clinton again in 1996.

But Arthur Laffer hasn't really gone too far off the conservative campus. He was an early and vociferous opponent of the public option proposal in the Obama health care plan. For instance, there was this comment on CNN: "If you like the post office and the Department of Motor Vehicles and you think they're run well, just wait until you see Medicare, Medicaid, and health care done by the government." That's red meat for the red states, isn't it?

Maybe so. But Arthur Laffer doesn't toe a predictable party line. He may have had official roles in a Republican government, but he's more economist than politician. His educational background in economics includes an undergraduate degree from Yale and a master's and PhD from Stanford. And he's been on the faculty at the University of Chicago, the University of Southern California, and Pepperdine University. He was called one of the twentieth century's greatest minds by *Time* magazine for his formulation of supply-side economics in 1974. So he might be able to think for himself, *especially* when it comes to economics.

He now believes that the flat tax is the direction the country should be going. "I love the flat tax," he says. He sees it somewhere around 13 percent, for individuals and businesses alike. And who is he working with to push this? California Attorney General Jerry Brown, who is running for governor.

That should stir things up again.

The one true irony of Arthur Laffer's career is that someone so brilliant could do something, well, not so brilliant. He talks about something he and another great mind, Milton Friedman, did together early in their careers.

Arthur Laffer's Best Mistake, in His Own Words

I joined the University of Chicago faculty in 1968. I came from Stanford. And I was the whiz kid, or so I thought.

There was a money workshop where Milton Friedman was complaining that he wanted to speculate against the dollar with the British pound. But at that time it was illegal to speculate against currencies in the United States.

International trade is my specialty, and I had read *The New York Money Market* by Margaret Meyers, which is a three-volume set on how the money markets and the forward markets (futures) were all developed from the currency markets and the commodities.

 What I told Milton was if you're trying to do a political point, that's fine, but if you *really want to speculate*, you can do it through commodities.

You can buy sugar forward [buy a futures contract expecting the price of sugar to go up] in the currency you want to short [the currency you want to bet against], and sell sugar forward in the currency you want to go long. Therefore, you've got a contract that's zero net in the commodity, and all you've done is shorted one currency and gone long the other.

[*Note:* You can bet on the price of sugar to go up or down, but it really doesn't matter where the price goes in this case because you're betting *both* sides of the transaction, so the contracts cancel each other out. If one sugar contract goes up, the other goes down the same amount.

But the currencies the contracts are bought and sold in will change. So you get rid of the currency you think is going to go down by *buying* the contract on sugar. (You're taking that currency out of your pocket and paying for the contract in that currency.) And you take in more of the currency you want to own by *selling* the sugar contract. (When you sell the contract, you take in that currency and put it in your pocket.) After the contracts expire, you're holding more of the currency you wanted in your pocket. Your belief is that the currency in your pocket will be worth more than the currency you took out of it to buy the contract.

All of this, of course, ignores any costs to own the contracts, or what it costs to borrow that money.]

So I'm into international trade—that's my specialty—so I explained it to Milton. And Milton said, "No, no, Arthur, you're wrong—it doesn't work that way."

So that night I get this phone call. "Hello, Arthur, Milton here. Could you go through that again?"

And I say, "Sure. If you want to go short the British pound and go long the German mark, what you do is buy sugar forward (futures) in pounds, because then you're selling pounds and buying sugar, and sell sugar forward in marks. You're going to give sugar up and *get* marks. So you've really shorted the pound and longed the mark. That's how you do it."

He thought that was great. And I set it up to do this.

Two things went wrong. The first thing was that Germany at that time did not have a sophisticated-enough currency market to have commodities like sugar traded in German marks. So I couldn't do it in the German mark.

I had to do it in the pound, but not in the German mark. So I did it on the pound and the dollar.

So I sold sugar forward in pounds, and I bought sugar forward in dollars. [*Note:* This would be a position to bet the British pound would go up and the dollar down.]

 The broker thought I was stupid. He said, "Let me see if I've got this right. You're selling sugar forward and you're buying sugar forward—is that right?" I said, "That's exactly right." He thought this was the dumbest thing he'd ever heard.

And I had done this with Milton. Milton put in his money, and so did I.

Then the second thing went wrong. The German mark *re*valued, so there was no effect on the pound and the dollar. So we missed it. But hey, that happens. At least we didn't lose any money, because we were evenly balanced.

But all of a sudden, I started getting margin calls. Why? I had matched the same number of tons with the same number of tons, so it shouldn't be a problem. But the broker came to me and said, "We're getting margin calls and I can't figure out why." And I couldn't figure out why, either.

Just so you know, this is a really stupid business mistake: The British contracts, the pound contracts, are done in British tons, and the U.S. contracts are done in U.S. tons.

 Two thousand pounds is a U.S. ton, and *2,240 pounds* is a British ton. And I had this *enormous* net position in sugar because I had it highly leveraged. And I lost my shirt and Milton's shirt at the same time!

Now, it wasn't a lot of money, because I was just an assistant professor, but can you imagine my embarrassment going to *Milton Friedman* explaining to him the mistake I made?

Q. What was the lesson?

Two things. Number one, to be a little bit more careful and actually work through examples. But number two, to have a little bit more humility—and find a broker who really knows what he's doing! Ha!

About Arthur Laffer

Arthur B. Laffer is the founder and chairman of Laffer Associates, an institutional economic research and consulting firm, as well as Laffer Investments, an institutional investment management firm utilizing diverse investment strategies. Laffer Associates' research focuses on the interconnecting macroeconomic, political, and demographic changes affecting global financial markets. Laffer Investments' investment management strategies utilize some of the economic principles and models pioneered by Dr. Laffer as well as other unique offerings managed by the firm's portfolio management group. The firms provide research and investment management services to a diverse group of clients, including institutions, pension funds, corporations, endowments, foundations, individuals, and others.

Dr. Laffer's economic acumen and influence in triggering a worldwide tax-cutting movement in the 1980s have earned him the distinction in many publications as "the father of supply-side economics." One of his earliest successes in shaping public policy was his involvement in Proposition 13, the groundbreaking California initiative that drastically cut property taxes in the state in 1978.

Years of experience and success in advising on a governmental level have distinguished Dr. Laffer in the business community as well. He currently sits on the board of directors of several public companies, which include: MPS Group Inc. (MPS) and Oxigene Inc. (OXGN). He also sits on the board of directors or board of advisers of a number of private companies, including Alpha Theory, Atrevida Partners, BAP Power, BridgeHealth Medical, F-Squared Investments, HealthEdge Partners, LifePics, Nicholas Applegate Institutional Funds, Pillar Data Systems, and Retirement Capital Group.

Dr. Laffer was a member of President Reagan's Economic Policy Advisory Board for both of his two terms (1981–1989). He was a member of the executive committee of the Reagan/Bush Finance Committee in 1984 and was a founding member of the Reagan Executive Advisory Committee for the presidential race of 1980. He also advised Prime Minister Margaret Thatcher on fiscal policy in the United Kingdom during the 1980s.

He was formerly the Distinguished University Professor at Pepperdine University and a member of the Pepperdine board of directors. He also held the position as the Charles B. Thornton Professor of Business Economics at the University of Southern California from 1976 to 1984. He was an associate professor of business economics at the University of Chicago from 1970 to 1976 and a member of the Chicago faculty from 1967 through 1976.

During the years 1972 to 1977, Dr. Laffer was a consultant to Secretary of the Treasury William Simon, Secretary of Defense Donald Rumsfeld, and Secretary of the Treasury George Shultz. He was the first to hold the title of chief economist at the Office of Management and Budget (OMB) under Mr. Shultz from October 1970 to July 1972.

Dr. Laffer has been widely acknowledged for his economic achievements. Recently he was noted in *Time* magazine's March 29, 1999, cover story, "The Century's Greatest Minds" for inventing the Laffer curve, which it deemed one of "a few of the advances that powered this extraordinary century." He was listed in "A Dozen Who Shaped the '80s," in the *Los Angeles Times* on January 1, 1990, and in "A Gallery of the Greatest People Who Influenced Our Daily Business," in the *Wall Street Journal* on June 23, 1989. His creation of the Laffer curve was deemed a "memorable event" in financial history by *Institutional Investor* in its July 1992 Silver Anniversary issue, "The Heroes, Villains, Triumphs, Failures and Other Memorable Events."

The awards that Dr. Laffer has received for his economic work include two Graham and Dodd Awards from the Financial Analysts Federation for outstanding feature articles published in the *Financial Analysts Journal*; the Distinguished Service Award by the National Association of Investment Clubs; the Adam Smith Award for his insights and contributions to the perpetuation of the ideals of a free market economy as first laid out in *The Wealth of Nations*; and the Daniel Webster Award for public speaking by the International Platform Association. Dr. Laffer also earned the Father of the Year award from the West Coast Father's Day Committee in 1983.

Dr. Laffer received a BA in economics from Yale University in 1963. He received a MBA and a PhD in economics from Stanford University in 1965 and 1972, respectively.

Read more at www.time.com/time/magazine/article/0,9171,990633-5,00 .html#ixzz0eZukslG4.

Chapter 30

DAVE RAMSEY

Host of syndicated *Dave Ramsey* radio show

2009 Marconi Award winner

Creator of Financial Peace University

W hen I walked into Dave Ramsey's office building, it smelled like cookies.

The building itself could have been the headquarters of a certified public accountant (CPA) or law firm, as professional as it was, but to the immediate left there was a bookstore.

It displayed all of the books that Dave Ramsey has published, as well as his motivational DVDs, board games that teach you how to manage your money, and select titles from other authors on how to get your life together—especially your financial life. There was a flat screen TV on the wall running one of Dave's speeches in front of an audience, where he lays out the steps to go from financial ruin to financial responsibility.

"May I get you something?" the lady behind the counter asked. "I just made a batch of cookies. Do you like chocolate chip?" As I recall my visit, she looked like June Cleaver. But it could be that my mind simply took a step back in time because I *wanted* her to look like the Beav's mother. There's something about Dave Ramsey's story, about his modest beginnings in Antioch, Tennessee, and his straightforward approach to helping people get out of debt and take control of their lives that speaks of a simpler time.

"I think what you're doing," he told me when I was escorted into his personal office, "is encouraging, because I believe the little man really *can* get ahead."

That's it. Forget the complicated financial schemes created by Wall Street financial experts that promised never-ending riches based on leverage and widely distributed risk—we all know where they got us. Dave Ramsey's story is heart-of-the-country Americana.

"America is the only place that has sanctified capitalism—capitalism done with morals," he continues. "It's the only system with the opportunity for the little man to get ahead. Socialism doesn't give the little guy the opportunity to get ahead. Communism certainly doesn't. So other methods or strains of economic thought do not lift people up. What lifts people up is opportunity, and then people deciding to go *take* it."

It's a philosophy that has convinced more than a million people to take his courses all the way from beginning to end, from personal financial collapse to fiscal control and the ability to sleep at night and get away from the nightmare of creditors hounding you day and night for what little money you may still have. Dave knows all about it.

You have that moment where you say, "Never again. Never again will I be beholden to a banker. Never again will American Express call my house and ask my wife why she would stay with a man who won't pay his bills. Never again am I going to be subject to that kind of abuse because of my own stupidity. Never again."

You can't fake that. The authenticity of Dave Ramsey's story rings true to his readers, viewers, and listeners (he's been on the radio for more than 17 years).

His story is a classic case of getting the most out of a mistake. But the lessons came hard. He says:

Pain is a thorough teacher. You don't forget. And the deeper the pain, the more thorough the lesson. It certainly is the mistake that has been the cornerstone of our story. Everybody's got a story. And it's the thing that allows us to relate our readers, our listeners, our viewers.

And in a classic quote from a wildly successful boy from middle Tennessee, he says, "I've done stupid with zeros on the end. I know what it looks like."

But while Dave Ramsey's approach is nonblinking, it's a little too easy to consider him just an average guy. It's one thing to get your financial life together and make your bank statement balance again, but it's quite another to build a self-help business empire based on it. He's got the radio program, a cable TV show, books, DVDs, speaking engagements—the whole works. And he's become a millionaire—twice. The first time he lost it all, and the second time he figured out how to hold on to it. But he wouldn't have succeeded the first time without the ability to do deals. He tells me he's always been a guy "who doesn't take no for answer," at least not without a fight. And that persistence has served him well as he's built his self-help business.

"I've met successful people all over the world," he says, "athletes, artists, and people who have huge ministries, people who are known on television or whatever, and we perceive those people's success as somehow being linear, from point A to point B, just a straight line up the mountain. And the truth is it's a whole life full of fits and starts. It's a life full of course corrections. It's a life full of bumps on the head so you learn where to not put your head again."

Dave Ramsey's story is a clear case of someone making the best out of their mistakes. And his business started with his best mistake.

"Everything we've done has been built on mistakes. We figured out that the gleaming mountain of success looks more like a pile of garbage. All you're doing is standing on it instead of lying under it. That's the only difference between being successful or not. This whole place is built on a series of errors. The way we run the organization—the core values that are written down— are the things that we did wrong and figured out how not to do anymore."

Dave Ramsey's Best Mistake, in His Own Words

I started with nothing when I was 22 years old. I got married and I was out of college and I started buying and selling real estate and got rich—at least by the standards of a kid from Antioch, Tennessee. I ended up with about $4 million worth, and about a million-dollar net worth.

We were going great guns, and I had borrowed a lot of money because I have a natural gift with deals and a natural gift with math, and I really don't accept no as an answer very often. Put those things together and I was able to talk my way into a ridiculous amount of debt. And those days were not unlike the days a couple years ago when bankers were throwing money at the Street. [This was starting in 1984 up to about 1986.]

Interest rates were high but coming down. We were seeing fixed rates in the 11 to 12 percent range, down from 17 percent. That was great. The real estate market was doing well. So I could go into a bank as a young go-getter, with a nice suit and a nice car, and show them the deals I had done, and talk them into loaning me more money. And I did. And if that banker turned me down, I could go talk to another one, because there was one on every corner.

So I had lines of credit or deal money all over town. All of it was aboveboard, but it was just ridiculous, honestly. For a 26-year-old kid to be able to go $3 million in debt, all for the fact that his dad used to be in the real estate business, and he's had a real estate license for a few years and he seems to be making money in these deals. . . . It enabled me, through my stupidity, to be able to build a house of cards, which is what it amounted to.

We had a lot of 90-day notes because we were "buying it, fixing it, and flipping it." That enabled the banks to call the notes. I didn't have a lot of long-term mortgages; I think we had fewer than 100 properties with long-term mortgages on them. Most of the stuff we had was flip stuff.

Then the tax law changed under President Reagan. And the savings and loan (S&L) failures were beginning. And as word of that stuff started hitting the street, and the bank that I was working with got sold—and it was the first time that a bank in Tennessee could be owned by a bank that was not chartered in Tennessee—suddenly for the first time we had the megabank in another city, 500 miles away, looking over a portfolio that they just bought.

They looked at that and said, "There's a kid that's 26 who owes us a million bucks here. What the heck's going on?" And they freaked out. And they just came in with a hatchet to clean up, and I was one of the branches. So they called our notes.

And I had 90 to 100 days to come up with a million bucks, and in real estate, that doesn't work. Had we been given the time, say over two years, to work out these properties—we had plenty of equity in them—we could have done it. We were not losing money; we were making money hand over fist.

But I had left myself vulnerable because of my arrogance.

There was no exit strategy—it was all up!

It was 1986 when they called the notes. We spent the next two and a half years fighting, and trying to do the right thing and pay the bills. My income was $250,000 one year, and the next year my taxable income was $6,000.

I spent the whole year selling stuff trying to meet the obligation. By the time we got to the bottom we owed less than $400,000—two and a half years later—from $3 million. But by then the lawsuits had stacked up and they were well on down the pike, and they were literally coming on Friday morning to get the furniture out of our house (they had gotten a judgment and they were collecting assets to try to pay the bill). And we had a brand-new baby. And it was a fairly small bill on that particular lawsuit, only about 20 thousand bucks. But it didn't matter. The furniture was probably only worth 15 hundred, but I was out of emotional energy. I had done all I could do.

So we drove a stake in the ground and filed bankruptcy that Thursday afternoon to keep them from coming that Friday morning—September 23rd of 1988. That's the splat. You jump off a cliff, you go splat.

So, millionaire at 26, bankrupt at 28.

I'd like to tell you that I bounced back, but I really didn't. I sat around whining and blaming everybody else for a while. It was everybody else's fault. It was the bank's fault. It was the IRS's fault. It was Congress's fault for changing the laws. It was everybody else's fault but mine. It couldn't be my fault.

It couldn't be the obvious, that I'm the klutz. It took a while. And that was an emotional, relational, and spiritual growth to the point of owning that, to the point of saying, "I'm the one who put my family in jeopardy. My decisions did that."

Following that, you have that moment where you say, "Never again."

So I went on a quest to find out how money really works. Because obviously the plan I had didn't work. It's kind of like a Dr. Phil moment: "How's that working for you?" It's not!

And I discovered common sense talking to old rich people. And I saw a bunch of common threads, and as a Christian I discovered that the biblical financial principles really are common sense. There's nothing mystical there.

One of the things we discovered was that debt is really a pretty dumb idea. In spite of all the sophisticated nonsense that flies around, with fairly naive mathematical formulas, pitching what a good idea it is, at the end of the day Warren Buffett doesn't like debt. He says it's the number one thing that keeps people from building wealth. And that's probably a guy you ought to listen to.

I just figured out that most wealthy people avoid debt like the plague. And why is it that they're able to avoid debt but the middle class isn't? And the middle class stays middle class. And I discovered a trend. If you want to be skinny, do what skinny people do. And if you want to be rich, do what rich people do. It's not a hard program.

At the end of the day, people who are icons in business, dotted across the American landscape, don't like debt. And it's one of the reasons they got where they are, because it keeps risk out of your life. And it keeps your most powerful wealth-building tool in your control, which is your income. When you commit that to somebody else, you don't have any money.

So we started leaving debt out of our lives and the healing then began. We started living those things as just a pain-avoidance mechanism, if nothing else. And my wife Sharon and I slow-w-w-w-ly started putting our lives back together.

Then I started teaching a Sunday school class on the subject, and there were ministry people in our church who were in foreclosure and the struggling preacher didn't know what to do with them—preachers aren't good with money usually.

He'd call me up and I'd go sit down with them and help them do a budget and help them save their foreclosure and that kind of stuff, and it evolved slowly into a business, with speaking and teaching.

 Then on a lark I went on this radio program as a guest. Then the guy quit and I talked the guy that ran the radio station into putting me on for free.

Q. Did you go back into real estate and just do it in a different way?

Yes, I didn't have any choice. I had two kids to feed and I didn't know what else to do. It was the only skill set I had. I can either dig ditches or I can do this. It's what I know how to do.

So I would go dig up a deal on a house, a great bargain, contract for it subject to a partner's agreement, and then go to all my old competitors who used to bid against me for foreclosure deals, and then sell it to them, and make a spread. Even though I didn't have credit I knew how to put together deals, and I knew how to find them, and I work harder than anybody else.

It took a while. My confidence was shattered. I didn't *believe* I could do anything. But I was too scared to do anything else, because I had to keep the lights on and these babies fed. I didn't know what else to do, so I was just running.

A little desperation is good for the soul, but a lot of it's not.

Q. How did you expand your self-help business, besides helping people at church?

We started syndicating the radio show. We were just taking calls from hurting people.

Q. How did you know enough to handle the variety of questions?

When I started out I was doing real estate deals and I bought and sold foreclosures. So I knew foreclosures inside and out. And then I had been a foreclosure. [*Laughs.*] And in bankruptcy, it was the same thing. I had worked the bankruptcy courts, buying deals out of there, so I knew the law and the way the stuff worked in the courts. That's the way I made my money. And I was buying deals. Anywhere I could find a deal I'd scratch it up. So I knew how the banks thought; I knew how the foreclosures worked; I knew the laws. I had worked that for almost a decade—a lot of hours, a lot of deals.

So I learned that side of the business, and then I went through it personally and that gave me another decent set of information on the business. And dealing with collectors—I got to deal with them personally.

And there have been changes over the years, but thank goodness we're not just a radio show, or otherwise we probably wouldn't have the expertise. But I've got a building full of people who do this stuff every day. We've got some four or five thousand counselors nationwide that we have trained and that are in the field giving us feedback all the time, too. So we've got our finger on the pulse of what's going on.

About Dave Ramsey

A personal money management expert, Dave Ramsey is an extremely popular national radio personality and best-selling author of *The Total Money Makeover*, *Financial Peace*, and *More Than Enough*. He is also host of *The Dave Ramsey Show* on the Fox Business Network. Ramsey knows firsthand what financial peace means in his own life—living a true rags-to-riches-to-rags-to-riches story. By age 26 he had established a $4 million real estate portfolio, only to lose it by age 30. He has since rebuilt his financial life and now devotes himself full-time to helping ordinary people understand the forces behind their financial distress and how to set things right. Through his proven plan, Ramsey helps people eliminate debt and credit cards, learn to budget, avoid bankruptcy, build wealth, and find financial peace.

Ramsey founded the Lampo Group, Inc. to provide financial counseling, through various means, to the public. More than one million families have completed Financial Peace University, with the typical family saving $2,700 and paying off $5,300 of debt. More than 650,000 people have attended a Dave Ramsey live event. Ramsey created Financial Peace Jr. to help parents teach sound financial principles to their children. Active in more than 5,000 schools in all 50 states, Foundations in Personal Finance educates high school students on the importance of financial planning and the dangers of debt. Ramsey's syndicated newspaper column, *Dave Says*, is read by nearly five million readers weekly. *The Dave Ramsey Show* is syndicated to more than 450 radio stations nationwide with more than 4.5 million weekly listeners. *The Dave Ramsey Show* on the Fox Business Network launched October 15, 2007.

Conclusion

f you have read some or all of these profiles, I hope they've had the same effect on you as they've had on me. I somehow feel less like a loser to discover that even the most esteemed business leaders make mistakes. Yet in an interesting paradox, I also find myself more impressed. I came away with more respect for them since their career tracks weren't cleared for them like curling players sweeping the path of the stone on its way to the house. They succeeded not just despite the roadblocks they encountered, but in many cases *because* of them.

Since many of these business leaders are good managers, part of their success may be due to their ability to *manage* a mistake. As former Heisman Trophy winner turned businessman John Cappelletti told me, good managers are solving problems every day. Those problems really never stop coming, whether ones of their own making, those of their employees, or perhaps ones from the marketplace. Overcoming and dealing with problems is part of their ongoing task set and it's quite possible that a mistake, even one that can threaten a career, is encountered as just another problem to solve on the way to achieving career or personal goals.

Perhaps the smartest way to turn a mistake into a potentially positive situation is to change your perception of it. **Mistakes can be agents of change.** And such change can be for good or bad. The bad mistakes are the ones we would probably like to forget, and the good ones can affect our lives and/or careers in a positive way. Like self-made billionaire R. J. Kirk said, you can't learn from success. "With success you don't get feedback." But time after time in this book we saw careers and lives affected by mistakes that in retrospect turned out to be turning points.

Mistakes can change a career path. Mark Cuban was happy with the prospect of being a bar owner in Bloomington, Indiana. But his misstep put him on track to become an entrepreneur in the computer services field. In the long run his bank account was the clear beneficiary, as were the fans of the Dallas Mavericks.

Jim Buckmaster of Craigslist was going to be a doctor. Who wouldn't want that life of widespread respect and privilege? Well, *he* didn't, so he dropped out of medical school. His perceived mistake took him in a different career direction that suited him better.

And Bill Gross, the "Peter Lynch of bonds," was so drawn to blackjack that he became an expert at assessing risk. And where does that come in handy? Managing a portfolio of bonds.

Mistakes can summon creativity. William O'Neil was a decent stock picker, and was pretty good at knowing when to buy a stock. But his mistake pushed him to figure out when to *sell* a stock—the second part of the transaction. He did the research and put together an investing strategy called CAN SLIM that is followed by serious stock traders even today. And in an effort to distribute the pertinent information to execute that strategy, he created *Investor's Business Daily*.

Realtor Barbara Corcoran messed up twice—first by sending to the *New York Times* an average price of the apartments she had for sale, and then by creating videos of the properties' interiors. The first mistake led to the *Times* looking to her to provide real estate information for the entire city of New York—which she quickly assembled—and the second led to an advantage on the Internet that her competitors couldn't match for years.

Mistakes can create opportunities. Look at the legendary Jack Bogle. He miscalculated the politics on the board of directors at the Wellington Group and got pushed out as chief executive of the company. They told him he couldn't manage money anymore. So he went off and created the stock index mutual fund. Just about every 401(k) in the country has benefited from that mistake, as has the company he started up, Vanguard, to offer the new product.

Jack Welch, *Fortune* magazine's "Manager of the Century," thought he was going to be fired after his mistake (blowing the roof off a building!). Instead, he established a relationship with a superior that was pivotal in his career advancement. That was an opportunity he conceivably wouldn't have had otherwise.

Mistakes can force you to up your game. Peter Lynch actually committed a mistake by taking a big profit on a stock. The problem was he could have made a *bigger* profit. So he developed a better way to monitor the progress of a company's development and in turn its stock value.

Jim Cramer became a better hedge fund manager after he and his partner made some serious investment missteps. He made a mistake, corrected it, and saved the firm. Arthur Blank learned a lesson and helped The Home Depot grow beyond the wildest expectations of Wall Street.

While some mistakes are better than others, **there are also mistakes that aren't really mistakes at all.** You could even say that it's kind of a copout when a participant in the book describes an incident as a mistake when they made a decision that everybody else thought was wrong but they knew was not. But to be fair, we should ask the question: Did they know for sure that it wasn't a mistake *at the time?* Probably not.

Meredith Whitney chose to step away from Wall Street, and everybody thought she had been fired. She eventually returned and made the call on bank stocks heard up and down the Street. Ian Bremmer decided he wanted to leave the cushy confines as a professor at Stanford University and start up a business with no guarantee of success. His employees, who now gather valuable information and provide analysis for investment companies on Wall Street and politicians inside the Beltway, are spread throughout the world. Danny Wegman made a business decision that cost his company $12 million, but he felt it was the right thing to do as a recession began to take hold. Wegmans Food Markets are once again considered among the best places to work in the United States.

These successful business leaders all followed a gut feeling that guided them to make a decision contrary to everyone else's expectations. It's a common thread in many of the book's stories. And there was no case in which someone told me they regretted following that inner voice. On the contrary. Suze Orman failed to follow hers one time and it cost her about a million dollars. She'll emphatically recommend staying loyal to that gut feeling in all your dealings, business or personal.

Steve Forbes ignored his father's advice and published a business magazine in college. Arianna Huffington ignored warnings of even her closest friends and associates and went ahead with the HuffingtonPost.com. Dr. Bill Frist said good-bye to Harvard and followed his gut to the West Coast, to learn about heart transplants from a man who was considered a pioneer, but also an iconoclast. The organ transplant center at Vanderbilt University was the eventual beneficiary of Frist's decision.

But that's not to say that there isn't a cost to following that inner voice. Jim Buckmaster may have ended up rich when he went from programmer to

CEO at Craigslist, but he spent 10 years wondering whether he had made the right decision to follow his gut.

David Novak, CEO of Yum! Brands, followed his commitment for a new Pepsi product because he knew it was the right thing to do. But he ignored Pepsi franchisees at his own peril. He learned a painful lesson that informs his business decisions now. He still follows that inner voice, but he listens to a few outer ones, too.

Given the positive results that can occur when someone is visited by a misstep, it's hard to believe that mistakes are given such a bad rap. Would we know who some of these people are if they hadn't messed up?

Would Dave Ramsey be a household name to the millions of families looking for help to get a handle on their finances? Would Arianna Huffington be as well known if she hadn't suffered a humiliating public moment? Would anybody listen to Peter Lynch if he hadn't designed an approach to investing that not only succeeded on the bottom line but made such common sense?

The participants in this book are widely respected business leaders and personalities who have earned the right to have their stories followed. I would never claim to deserve such attention. However, in anticipation of the natural question, "What was *your* best mistake, Bob?," I've enclosed a final story of my own.

It's another case of following your gut. What nobody tells you is that sometimes following that gut feeling can cause quite a stomachache.

In the late 1980s, I was living in the South Bay section of Los Angeles and I created a small alternative sports newspaper that combined an irreverent look at sports while giving the reader a forum for his or her own views. It was called the *L.A. Sports Rag*. (*Rag* in this case a double entendre, as "to give someone a hard time" and "a printed publication not worthy of your respect.") It was a great Internet idea, but it was before Al Gore had gotten around to inventing it. I lost every dime—and more—that I put into it.

Out of money and in need of work, I interviewed and got a job at Merrill Lynch as a financial consultant (stockbroker) in the Brentwood, California, branch. It was a four-month-long training program, which culminated in a three-week session back at training headquarters in Princeton, New Jersey. During the last week of training, I discovered that there was no trip to the stock exchange floor planned for the training class, which struck me as crazy. How was I supposed to talk to potential clients about what was happening on the stock exchange if I'd never been there? Besides, I had spent a good deal of time trading stock options during the mid-1980s and always wondered what the floor was like.

So I made a few phone calls and arranged to have a visit to the floor coordinated by some Merrill Lynch folks. I wasn't alone in wanting to go—a female colleague of mine from the same branch office went along as well. We took the train from Princeton to New York and made the trek down to lower Manhattan and to the bastion of American capitalism known as the New York Stock Exchange. I should mention that to do this, we had to skip a cold-calling class, which was to simulate the process we would officially begin the following Monday by calling prospects on a lead list and asking them to invest in my—or Merrill Lynch's—recommendations.

We had a great time. The floor was lit up like Las Vegas, without the waitresses serving free drinks, and it was thrilling to be in the middle of it all. The energy was intoxicating. I met floor brokers and spoke with specialists who created markets in listed stocks traded around the world. I asked questions about the trading process, examined their trading books, and learned about how important it was for them to know chart patterns and technical trading trends as they were obligated to buy or sell securities that could be proffered by individuals or institutions. What an education. It was infinitely more valuable than making cold calls, which I had made for many years in different sales positions.

But, as happens in so many joyful stories, then came the next morning. On the day we were preparing to return home from Princeton, I was in my colleague's hotel room when she got a call from our branch manager back in Los Angeles. He said that he heard about our trip to the stock exchange and that we had brought shame upon the branch. And she was fired. She was also told that when she saw me, she was to tell me that I'm fired, too. I figured I couldn't be fired by a co-worker—didn't a boss have to be involved?—so when the phone rang back in my own hotel room, I didn't answer it.

The rumors were swirling around the training class, including a story that blamed our unceremonious termination on an amorous escapade on a billiards table in the recreational wing of the Princeton facility. It wasn't true, but stories—especially juicy ones—tend to take on a life of their own.

On the following Monday I went back to the branch office in Brentwood. I thought that perhaps time and common sense would have imposed themselves upon the reactionary fervor of my boss so that we could all just have a good laugh and proceed to build a book of clients. No such luck.

When he saw me he said, "What are you doing here?"

"Working," I answered.

He flicked his hand dismissively, "Get out." That was the extent of our conversation. No good laugh ensued.

When I called a local branch manager with Shearson Lehman Hutton to see if I could interview for a job with him, he found it hard to believe a brokerage house like Merrill Lynch would go through the expense of training somebody for four months and then fire them for such a tame offense. Merrill even imposed a legal obligation on you that if you left within two years, you would pay back a prorated amount equal to the value of that training, and now I was allowed to walk away without owing a dime. The Shearson manager agreed to interview me on one condition. "Only if you tell me what really happened." So I brought up the billiards story.

Now, as Bill Cosby used to say after a long tale about Fat Albert before continuing with his "Buck Buck" story, "the reason I told you that story is to tell you this one."

It didn't take me long to realize I loved stocks, and I loved talking about company stories and investment opportunities, but I didn't love making a hundred cold calls a day trying to build a book of clients. I didn't have one brother who was a lawyer and another who was a CPA funneling clients my way as our top broker did.

Eventually I had had enough. So I followed my gut. I went in one day and told my branch manager I quit. It was a risky thing for me to do. I had no money. I had no career. I had no future. But my gut was telling me to stop doing what I was doing.

The one thing I *had* done that made some sense was send a homemade videotape to a local UHF television station that called itself the Business Channel. They were doing what FNN—which became CNBC—was doing, but on a more local level. Out of the blue, they called me. If I had still been working as a broker, I wouldn't have been available.

After a couple of auditions, the news director said he wanted to use me as a backup anchor and had me trained to use the computer system. After a month or so I was ready to go on the air, but I never got the call. When I followed up, it turned out the news director had been fired. The new career I thought I was about to embark upon had died before it started.

Since I could always type, I went to work as a Remedy temp. I was getting coffee for executives and typing up their interoffice memos. I was taken out to lunch for Secretary's Day and wondering what the heck I was going to do to build some kind of career that offered access to a bigger stream of income than $12 an hour. Don't get me wrong: I appreciated the paycheck. However, it seemed like I might have more to offer, but I didn't have a clue exactly what or where that would be.

I started writing humorous opinion pieces and sending them to the *Marketplace* program on public radio, which started using them. I recall one being about mergers and acquisitions being so prevalent that they had reached families, where big families would take over smaller families and—business being business—they would sometimes lead to layoffs of six-year-olds who were draining resources and not carrying their weight in T-ball.

Then the Business Channel called. The *new* news director wanted me to come in and anchor a show for someone who was out for a week. My TV career had begun.

I have since worked for two decades in television, anchoring and reporting on the local level as well as for national cable networks. I followed an unknown candidate for governor in Texas and watched him win there and then make his way to the White House. I've anchored election-night coverage during presidential races too close to call and in 2003 traveled to Iraq to report on events following the "end of combat hostilities." It was a period I describe as going from the honeymoon phase to the "Washington, we have a problem" phase. I was reporting on Wall Street for CNBC during the dot-com bubble and collapse, and working in Washington, D.C., when an African American made history by taking the oath of office as president of the United States.

There are many other television people who have had better and more lucrative careers, but I consider myself blessed to have experienced mine. At a certain point in Los Angeles I had nowhere to go and was on the verge of living in my car—but a friend let me sleep in her closet. To do the things I've ended up doing in journalism was just a dream at that point.

I think it's fair to say that if I hadn't worked at the national level, especially at CNBC, I never would have had the privilege of talking to the people in this book and putting these profiles in print. And if the stories here inspire somebody in some way, I'll consider it time well spent.